T0208914

Concepts, Ideas, and Values for Your Life

words
to
live
by

JAMES FREY

BALBOA.
PRESS
A DIVISION OF HAY HOUSE

Balboa Press books may be ordered through booksellers or by contacting:

Balboa Press
A Division of Hay House
1663 Liberty Drive
Bloomington, IN 47403
www.balboapress.com
1 (877) 407-4847

Because of the dynamic nature of the Internet, any web addresses or links contained in this book may have changed since publication and may no longer be valid. The views expressed in this work are solely those of the author and do not necessarily reflect the views of the publisher, and the publisher hereby disclaims any responsibility for them.

The author of this book does not dispense medical advice or prescribe the use of any technique as a form of treatment for physical, emotional, or medical problems without the advice of a physician, either directly or indirectly. The intent of the author is only to offer information of a general nature to help you in your quest for emotional and spiritual well-being. In the event you use any of the information in this book for yourself, which is your constitutional right, the author and the publisher assume no responsibility for your actions.

Any people depicted in stock imagery provided by Getty Images are models, and such images are being used for illustrative purposes only.
Certain stock imagery © Getty Images.

Print information available on the last page.

ISBN: 978-1-9822-0332-0 (sc)
ISBN: 978-1-9822-0333-7 (hc)
ISBN: 978-1-9822-0389-4 (e)

Library of Congress Control Number: 2018905438

Balboa Press rev. date: 05/07/2018

Jim Frey's "Words to Live By" – a collection of inspirational, motivational words, thoughts, and quotes meant to make you think, reflect, smile, even laugh a bit; helpful, useful stuff to make your life better.

To the reader; I am grateful that you are taking time to read this book, thank you. It means a lot to me. The content is important to me. I believe that there is true wisdom in its pages – and I don't say that because I wrote it, it is because the thoughts and ideas enclosed are found out in the world. I don't claim to own or create this wisdom. In many cases, the ideas are things that you may already be familiar with – but like many good things in life, we need to be reminded and we need to practice.

This book was created for others with the best of intentions in mind. I love to learn and I love to teach. I find joy in helping others in different ways. As you will read in the *Forward*, these "Words" were created first for my daughters, then for me, and now I am grateful that I get to share them with you and many others.

The book was set up so that you can read about and focus on one "Word" per day through out the month. Ponder it, use it, focus on it, and integrate it into your life in your own way. Each "Word" starts with a formal definition, then three relevant quotations on that "Word", then my informal definition of the "Word", followed by my commentary and thoughts. Some "Words" have a bonus article, video or other. If you like the quotes, you will find more in the back of the book.

Foreword

In 1998, my wife, Jill, and I learned that we were expecting our first child. Like many parents we were excited, maybe a little intimidated, and certainly very grateful for being able to have a child. We enjoyed the experience all the way.

One day at work, I had a moment to reflect on the pregnancy and my soon-to-arrive child. I was excited but I began to wonder if I could prepare or do anything better than just wait for the arrival.

You see, I am someone who constantly reads and looks for ways to improve. I don't say this to impress you – in fact it's probably a neurotic sort of tendency. No matter what people say to compliment me, no matter what position I have in life, I always try to improve it. Some of this is self-help, some of this is spirituality, but it certainly goes well beyond that.

So I asked myself, "What else can I do to prepare my child (or children) for the world?" I knew that life goes rather quickly and that there are many distractions. I thought about school, religion, politics, and life.

I always felt that my parents gave me a great up bringing; not only by what they did for me but what they had me do for myself. I tried to think about what they did and said. It came down to teaching me values and beliefs. I recall both parents telling me about honesty, what someone's word means, integrity, hard work, courage, and beliefs. This was a good start, I thought, but all of the things they offered was verbal. How could I pass this down? How could I be sure that the message was thorough and consistent?

I also thought that, in a child's life, who really teaches them about life, about religion, spirituality, and wisdom? From age 0 to 18, who do they spend the most time with and what values do they learn during that time? School offers education. Religion offers some values and morals. Parents contribute much of it, sometimes intentionally, sometimes accidentally. Where do our children really learn values? Observing us? Is it always clear to them how we feel about something? Is there a way to be clearer?

I suppose that I slept on this for a day or so and then it occurred to me that I could create some sort of dictionary like book with values that are important to my wife and me. We could literally spell them out and pass this information to our kids.

My wife started to get a little more tired each night because of the pregnancy, understandably so. She might go to bed early or drift on the couch next to me. I was someone who stayed up late. I took this time to start this 'dictionary of values' – I was still looking for the name.

I started by looking up words in a real dictionary so that I could begin with their real meanings. I then created my own 'definition' and sometimes added my own examples, thoughts, or comments.

My first daughter, Emma, was born in early July 1999. We celebrated her birth and really enjoyed all of it. I found that people would tell me things like, "Just wait until you try to sleep…." Or "Just wait until they turn two – the terrible two's" and "Just wait until she grows up – ugh, a teenage girl." and other sorts of things that weren't really that positive. I thought that this is also some of the stuff that I want to discuss with my children in my book; How expectations, attitude, perception, beliefs, stories can all affect your life.

As it turned out, we really didn't experience the bad stuff like many said – the 'terrible two's', or even the crazy teenage years like many described. Sure, life had its challenges, ups and downs, and nothing was perfect but I think our attitude really made things go nicely for us. I have enjoyed every moment with my daughters and with my wife.

Not too much later, we found out that we were expecting our second child. I began to write more and one day it suddenly came to me that, I'm giving my kids 'words for them to live by.' So I named this ever-growing book "*Words To Live By*."

Abby arrived in November 2000, and again, we enjoyed everything around our daughters. We did decide to pause before more kids, so that we could spend the desired time with them, on our careers, and with each other. One never knows if it is the right decision but it was our decision.

I continued to add more *Words*, fine-tune others, and off and on, it grew. I changed jobs and life happened.

When they were around six and seven years old, I had a bright idea to turn "*Words To Live By*" into a workbook. I took it to a copy shop, put one *Word*, along with its definition, on each page, leaving a large blank space underneath. I had them bind the book with a coil so that it could be opened on a table and easily used by two small, cute, girls.

After dinner and on long car trips we would spend time on a *Word* or two. We'd talk about it, ask the girls what they thought, and then ask them to write down some notes and draw pictures with crayons and markers. Often I found myself going into it like the all-knowing teacher. Then the girls would say something that I didn't think of and I found that I was learning just as much as they were.

As a side benefit, I really got to learn more about what my wife thought on these values. It wasn't that our beliefs were much different but we never really sat and talked about honesty, action, and other things like that. We all were communicating and growing together and it seemed like we all had a good time.

The girls really made some great pictures and notes. We still have those coloring books. I still look through them and I'm amazed at what they put down at such a young age. We made some great memories together.

Years later, my wife would mention it to someone or I'd bring it up on a rare occasion. Overall, it began to fade from daily life. As my daughters grew and school activities increased, we let life get in the way and we got away from the "*Words To Live By*" sessions. I think a part of me was also afraid as teens, they wouldn't like it, and I didn't want to turn them off either. I wanted them to have good memories and pursue it on their own.

In 2009, one of the tough years in my life came along. The nation was reeling from the Great Recession – or whatever label you wish to give to that period of 2008-2009. I was in banking – small business lending to be exact – and the bank that I worked for had put a large stake into an online-based mortgage-lending platform. Their timing was unfortunate and they lost millions – hundreds of millions I'm told.

Like many companies, they decided to downsize. They closed our division and two others – even though we weren't part of the problem nor were we doing 'sub-prime' transactions. Seven hundred fifty of us lost our jobs in December of 2008. Certainly, I began to send our resumes and do a job search but I had never found it difficult to find a job before, so I wasn't working too hard during the holidays.

January 2009 came and we lost my wife's maternal grandmother, a wonderful lady who I considered my 'surrogate grandmother." My grandparents were much older and I lost them years before. Many people felt the same way about Gram. She was a loving and wise person who always was ready to make you something good to eat.

A few months after, I went on a job interview to a former employer. I was feeling upbeat. I had the interview and was driving in my car. It was a beautiful, clear, cool day with lots of sunshine. I was feeling good. I got one phone call that my father was playing softball in Sarasota, as he often did. ……..

You see, my parents went away to Sarasota for four to five months each year to escape the Pennsylvania winter weather. They would ride bikes each day and meet friends – they acted like college students in the best sense of the word. My father typically played volleyball five days a week and softball twice. My parents were always going to some party, 'pot-luck' or some activity. My father was always playing some practical joke on someone, occasionally catching hell from the victim, and my mother. Still it kept them young, active and I believe it all made them live longer, and better lives.

To get back to that day, my father had ridden his bicycle to the ballfield as he did so many times before. I often imagine all of these sixty, seventy, and eighty year olds running around like some geriatric version of the movie "Sand Lot". Dad was playing softball and I'm told he had four good hits. He got up to home plate for his next at-bat. I understand that he was joking with someone, laughed, then coughed, then suddenly went down. A few guys performed CPR on him and the ambulance arrived incredibly fast. Still, after multiple other heart attacks and open-heart surgeries in his life, my father was gone.

The next day my sister and I here in Pennsylvania flew down to meet my Florida-based sister and mother. We helped her close up their place there and we all flew back to Pennsylvania together.

We had the funeral and experienced all that goes into that sort of life event. I remember that the funeral home viewing was actually such a nice experience, although sad. So many of my friends, and so many of my parents' friends came and said such nice things. They were sincere for their love for my father and we all spoke of the life he lived. We even had some gags, jokes, and a false plastic hand he used to prank people there in the funeral home as a reminder of his humor.

We spent time with my mother and found she needed hip surgery just a week or so later. Another week or so, we found out that the breast cancer that she beat in 1999 was back. It sounded more aggressive. I think my mother knew for some time and kept it from us. She started some radiation and treatments but soon we all learned that it was much too aggressive.

Five weeks after my father passed, my mother also passed away.

Again, the outpouring of support at the funeral home was wonderful and loving, but this time it did indeed seem sadder. I found some people, certainly myself, didn't know how to really process it all yet. I remember attending both of their funerals and wanting to say something, give a speech, share stories. However, I suppose I felt too wounded. On top of their deaths, I was still unemployed and feeling more desperate. I didn't feel like myself.

That year went on and it was tough to remain positive. My wife's uncle passed away from cancer in his early fifties. A few months later, her paternal grandmother passed away too. I continued to remain unemployed and my venture into self-employment was not going well. I had debts from an investment property that wasn't going well and our living expenses were too high. I couldn't seem to do anything right.

I reflected on a lot of things that year and I decided to start looking up quotes or upbeat things each day just to keep myself positive and from being depressed. I needed to change my attitude and I knew that it would take a while to dig myself out of the hole that I was in….

I got interested in starting a blog, just to post random interesting articles and these positive thoughts that I was trying find each day, so I tried a few versions and came up with something with some quotes. Sometimes I would add an article, a link or a TED Talk. It was random and progressing. I thought that there might be some discipline in posting it on a routine basis and that sharing good stuff might somehow produce other good things.

Eventually I had two versions; I started to have a blog post for each "*Word To Live By*" and a separate blog post with quotes, which I initially called "*Simple Stuff*". People started to give me positive feedback on the blog and I enjoyed the comments.

Time went on, things got better with my job and income. I began to heal from the crazy year of 2009. Eventually I combined the "*Words To Live By*" and the "*Simple Stuff*" and came up with something very similar to what is now the "*Frey Freyday*" email/ blog format. I continued to get positive feedback from friends and strangers all around the world. In particular, there were a handful of friends and a few of my wife's cousins that were always positive and supportive – and still are to this day. It is hard to quantify how one word of sincere positive feedback means to me, especially during those few tough years.

Years later I found myself in a job and with an employer that was very undesirable. It was a mistake for me to go there and I couldn't get out quick enough. I was unhappy. For a period of time I became very negative and upset. I wanted to withdraw and give up. Then I realized that I wanted to choose a better way, I wanted to be happy regardless. I wanted to have the best attitude that I could muster and put forth my best efforts. So, I spent time doing searches and I created blogs for 'good stuff' each day, it helped me stay focused and helped remind me that, regardless where I was in life, I needed to stay happy, positive and focused. And guess what, I connected to another job that I wanted and I connected to positive people. I believe that I found this new job because of my happy, elevated state of mind.

I started emailing a version of the blog posts to a few friends and clients. I got good feedback. Soon people started telling others, "Hey, do you get Jim's *Frey Freyday's*?", so the list slowly grew. Today I still try to post a blog and email each Friday with the "*Word To Live By*" and corresponding quotes – in other words, I pick a theme and all items offer a congruent thought. I do miss some Fridays for various reasons but I'm pretty consistent. I still get good feedback.

It is interesting to reflect; the purpose initially was, and still is, to explain to my daughters values and guidance.

Yet as I reviewed the words and quotes myself, and as friends and strangers read the blogs and emails, we all were reminded of important values and beliefs.

I believe that some of these "Words" and quotes and thoughts are simply truths, universal ideas and plain old wisdom. Most of the things I write about are not earth-shaking new ideas. I'm just reminding myself and others of them.

So today the email list slowly grows and continues. The blog still gets readers and gets positive comments. People from all over the world read it. We are not talking millions of people but hundreds, and that's OK for now.

To some degree, there is some commonality or community of sorts for people who like these reminders and appreciate being focused on values and beliefs. I am grateful for this situation and for these people.

So why am I writing this book?

Many of those readers – friends and strangers – in some way or another suggested that I write a book using the *"Frey Freydays"* and *"Words To Live By"*.

Also, I think the movement for a book really started internally with me one day when I wrote a blog post about my father:

"My dad was a cabinetmaker, and a good one. He grew a business that he and my mother started into a large firm with 30 employees. That stopped when he had a heart attack in his forties. He sold the business and became a manufacturers' agent in that industry. Many years later, I was fortunate to join him and work with him in the kitchen, bath and cabinet industry. I am grateful for that.

The whole time we were in that industry we would get all sorts of wood samples; cabinet doors, stain samples, wood countertops, moulding, and all sorts of things. My father saved most of it, much to my mother's chagrin.

My father wanted to, and often did, use those random parts to make something for a friend, loved one or for the church. He made things out of the samples for our church, he made things for my sisters and I, for friends, and even for the local Masonic lodge. But when my parents died, I had to clean out a large barn they owned. Inside was such a large collection of these samples. He had been retired for years and wanted to use each sample to make something for someone. In some ways, he might even be considered a hoarder. In any case, the sheer volume hit me – he wanted to share all of this with friends and loved ones but died before he could. In some ways, it was sad and riveting.

I remember I spent a whole day in the barn sifting through countless, random door samples and wood items. It was getting overwhelming because even though I felt most of it was junk, all of this 'stuff' was all still emotionally charged with feelings of grief for my parents, especially my dad. I came home and went into my home-office. I was suddenly struck by a pile of articles, handwritten notes, ideas, and other things that I had been writing and collecting over the years. I realized that, like my dad, I was collecting all of these things which I felt were valuable so that I could do something creative to them and share them with my friends and loved ones. Instead of doing something to a piece of wood, I intended on doing something with the paper and the information for others. Yet, like my father's "stuff", it was just sitting there.

If I died and my daughters had to clean up my life, would they find all of these articles, notes and ideas unfinished?

In other words, my dad wanted to stain, finish and create a wood piece of furniture. I wanted to take an article or idea, finish it and pass along something valuable and meaningful to others. Same idea, different product. But I was waiting. I wasn't sending out my product."

Years ago my parents introduced me to books and programs by Wayne Dyer. I often think of this quote by Wayne Dyer: *"DON'T DIE WITH YOUR MUSIC STILL IN YOU."*

It is now time to share these ideas, values, beliefs and bits of wisdom with you. I am confident good things will come of it. I am also so grateful that I can. I encourage you to share what you have with the world,……start now!

<u>A message to my daughters</u>: (written many years ago)

You are the reason that I started this all…….for so many reasons I am grateful for that.

I am writing this to you, my children. I am your parent. Sometimes that is a wonderfully fun, rewarding job. Sometimes it is most difficult. There are things like your first steps, your first words, the first few cute things you say. Times when you score the goal, get the "A", paint the picture. There are the late nights, the crying, the tantrums, dirty diapers, puking. Times when you disobey, break the rules, or hurt my feelings. There are times when I sit back and watch you behave well or do something with that special spunk only you have. Times when I hold back tears of pride and joy because I feel lucky to be your parent. There are times when I have to be firm, to say no, to punish you.

Please remember that if I punish you or restrict your activities, it is not because I enjoy it, or because I want you to know that I am in control. I am making these decisions because I want to protect you, to help you make the right decisions, and to make you the best person you can be. I make those decisions because it is my responsibility. Sometimes parents know just what to do. Other times it is a complete guess. Most of the times it is somewhere in between. As a good parent, I must act in your best interest, or at least what I think that is.

God, nature, and natural law dictate that I need to provide guidance, even if you don't welcome it. There will be times when my decisions,may not be the best ones. I am human and in many situations, I am learning just as you are. We are growing together. We both can look back and say that decisions and situations could have been better. Please know that I did my best.

There are times when a parent has to act like a parent or like a friend. Many times we can act as either. Many times, it is not clear which is best. It is my responsibility to first be a parent, then a friend. Some parents try to be a friend first, sort of buddy-buddy. While I think this can be good, I think that it is better for me to be a parent until you reach young adulthood.

There are also times when I would like to give you what you exactly what you want, and to serve it on a silver platter. I would like to make life easy, painless, and without problems. I would love to shelter you from hard times, worry, poverty, embarrassment, and all the tough things in life. I would like to buy the cars, the clothes, and all the gadgets you want. Sometimes I want to just give you the money you need to buy those 'toys.' But I know that giving you something for nothing will not mean much, it may even harm you. By letting you suffer a little or work harder now and achieve it on your own, I know that I am doing you a better service than the disservice of giving you what you want without efforts.

Hunger is something you get in cases like this and hunger, no matter where you are in life, at any age, is often a good thing. I know that in my own life and those lives around me, when you work for something or work through something on your own, you gain much more and appreciate it better than if it is given to you. My parents gave me things, at times, that I overlooked or didn't appreciate. When I got it on my own, it meant everything.

When you start your adult life, there will be things that I could do to help you with finances, for instance. I could give money to you but you might gain much more if you earned and saved it on your own. Call it tough love, call it what you want, I am doing it because I know that you can achieve things without me, that I have faith in you, and that when you reach your goal, you will feel much better knowing that you did it on your own. I am trying to give you one of the best gifts there is; self-reliance and independence. Once you have these, you will feel in control and confident. Whatever your path in life, if you can rely on yourself and have self-confidence, you will be happy and succeed.

There will be times, especially as you reach the teenage years and adulthood, when you will reject my thoughts and suggestions, when you will think that I am 'uncool' and that I embarrass you. In many cases, you will choose the opposite of what I do or say and rebel, just because. That is fine. That is in fact, healthy. Most children do that to and with their parents. I expect you to do it. Yet, I still must act in your best interest, despite your protests.

There will be many situations, probably more and more as you become mature and older, when you will assume that your mother and I won't understand. Situations that you will think are entirely new and unique to you and you alone. Pressures, trends, fads, choices, embarrassments, humiliations, mistakes, lies, hurts, lost loves, gossips, exclusions, fights, zits, failures, bad hair days, and other circumstances that may seem like you are the only one to face something like this. You are not. We know about choices regarding sex, drugs, being cool, trying to dress well, having the right gadgets, doing well in school without looking too smart, doing well in sports, being funny, having people take you seriously, being nice to everyone but not hanging with the weird people, being like others yet being an individual.

The teenage years are difficult. Your peers and your friends can be mean, either intentionally or unintentionally. You may feel alone. There are times when you need to talk and you don't want us to be judgmental. When those times come up, you can talk to a group of trusted friends or you can talk to us. We understand that life can be difficult and even overwhelming at times. We can discuss things like two adults. Ask for help. I bet we faced something like it. Even if we didn't, sometimes just talking about it can help. We're here if you need us.

Why am I writing this? I believe that some parents are doing a poor job being parents. Before I say more let me point out that I think I am not perfect, I need to improve as well. I am not pointing the finger. It takes a lot of time and effort to do it right. Many of us don't know how or what makes a great parent. Some of us may know but may not put the correct things into action.

Again, parenthood takes a lot of effort. I think that it takes effort to be average. It takes a little more to be above average.

To be great, much effort and knowledge is required. Maybe this exercise is a step in that direction.

Because of you, I want to be a better parent each day. Maybe you can learn something from all of this so that your lives are happier and healthier. As I mentioned before, these are not my ideas, this is wisdom and truth from many others. Even if you grab a few things, a few Words here you'll benefit. You're already a lot further along, a lot more mature than I was at your age. I expect great things. Your mother and I have enjoyed every moment and we find you both delightful. We are so very grateful that you're in our lives.

Table of Contents

Action - \\'ak-shən\\ - the process or state of acting or of being active

Stop acting as if life is a rehearsal. Live this day as if it were your last. The past is over and gone. The future is not guaranteed. – *Dr. Wayne Dyer*

—

Infuse your life with action. Don't wait for it to happen. Make it happen. Make your own future. Make your own hope. Make your own love. And whatever your beliefs, honor your creator, not by passively waiting for grace to come down from upon high, but by doing what you can to make grace happen… yourself, right now, right down here on Earth.-**Bradley Whitford**

—

There are risks and costs to action. But they are far less than the long range risks of comfortable inaction.-**John F. Kennedy**

WORD TO LIVE BY:

Action – Action is superior to reaction. Taking action means taking control of the situation – really it means being proactive. Action is often superior to remaining passive. By taking action you are making a statement, you gain momentum, energy moves with you and you can accomplish things.

Taking an action means you have truly made a decision. Actions are rewarded with gains. With action you may have failure, but that is part of the education that we all get in life. Too often in today's society we don't take action because we avoid failure. Go out and take action – and it's OK to fail! Learn and take more action.

If you don't know what to do, take action. Don't wait for it to be perfect. It's about progress, not perfection. You are smart and special enough to figure it out.

I believe that action is everything.

Ideas, imagination and good intentions are necessary but without action, they are nothing. Lots of people know what to do but few people actually do what they know. There are many people educated, people with great ideas, people with skills that don't take action from time to time, including me, and that is a waste. There is a saying that 'knowledge is power'. I believe that it is potential power, unrealized. We must take action.

Success in any field comes from taking the initiative and following up… and then persisting and taking action on a consistent basis.

It's not what we do once in a while that makes us who we are, but what we do consistently.

Ask yourself, "What simple action could I take today to move toward a dream or towards success in my life?"

Simplify-[sim-pluh-fahy] – to make less complex or complicated; make plainer or easier

Life is really simple, but we insist on making it complicated. Confucius
—

Success is nothing more than a few simple disciplines, practiced every day. Jim Rohn
—

Simplify, simplify. Henry David Thoreau
—

WORD TO LIVE BY:

Simplify - Many times we over complicate things – or we think that the "right" solution only comes via a complicated solution. (Sometimes our egos even get in the way.)

Often the best solution is a simple one.

Life, projects, work and other things can be broken down into simpler chunks – if you have a large task that seems overwhelming, just break it down into simple steps and keep it simple, sweetheart.

Momentum -[moh-men-**tuh** m] – force or speed of movement; impetus, as of a physical object or course of events: the force as movement or energy build
—

If you have the guts to keep making mistakes, your wisdom and intelligence leap forward with huge momentum. Holly Near
—

Success comes from taking the initiative and following up… persisting… eloquently expressing the depth of your love. What simple action could you take today to produce a new momentum toward success in your life? Tony Robbins
—

Belief in oneself is incredibly infectious. It generates momentum, the collective force of which far outweighs any kernel of self-doubt that may creep in. Aimee Mullins

WORD TO LIVE BY:

Momentum – Take consistent, small steps so as to keep moving forward and keep building energy, positivity and success - and keep it simple.

If you want to be successful, find someone who has achieved the results you want and copy what they do. Also, one reason so few of us get/do/become what we truly want is that we never direct our focus in a concentrated way. Most people wander or drift their way through life, never deciding to focus on or master anything specific.

In almost all cases, past failures and frustrations were actually teaching each of us things and laying the foundation for the understandings that have created the new level of living and being we all now enjoy.

Therefore, if we want to direct and focus our lives, career, relationships, achievements, then we must take control of our consistent actions. It's not what we do once in a while that shapes our lives, but what we do consistently. It has been said that a real decision is measured by the fact that you've taken a new action. If there's no action, you haven't truly decided.

The path to success is to take massive, determined action. If you do this, you'll build serious momentum.

So, even in simpler terms, just decide what it is that you really want, look for a model to emulate, focus on that "thing", and start taking steps now.

You can take small, simple steps, now, ….today. Take pride and celebrate in the successes and steps. Be happy even if you face adversity, make a mistake or fail, because you've taken a step in the right direction and even though it doesn't seem like it, you're building momentum.

In my own life, I recall when I was unhappy with a number of things in my life – I first became aware of those things and honestly looked at myself, and I took responsibility for those things – not always easy to do. Then I started to tackle one thing at a time. Example: For my health, I decided to cut out diet sodas. Small but important. The next week I focused on cutting out sugar. The next week I focused on limiting 'bad' carbs.

All small steps but I felt good as I had more successes. When I had a failure, I didn't beat myself up, and neither should you. Guilt, shame, and embarrassment isn't useful and exists just because you're assigning a certain meaning to something.

You failed because you're human, just like everyone else. So what? Keep going! The failure you just experienced just gave you some education and wisdom.

So, after I did these small things over a few weeks – really each action by itself is nothing earthshaking – I found that I was feeling better for lots of reasons and I had these references of success. I built on them and added newer and bigger goals. More exercise, leaner healthier foods, etc. I was able to build momentum.

Had I jumped right into all of it at once, or jumped into a bigger goal, it would have been possible - but much harder. Since I was able to build momentum, I felt more confident and used that to keep me going. Don't overthink it.

Belief -[bə'lēf]- an acceptance that a statement is true or that something exists:

—

Envy comes from people's ignorance of, or lack of belief in, their own gifts.-Jean Vanier

—

Nothing great has ever been achieved except by those who dared believe that something inside them was superior to circumstances. – Bruce Barton

—

It's not the events of our lives that shape us, but our beliefs as to what those events mean.-Tony Robbins

WORD TO LIVE BY:

Belief – Your beliefs make up your personality. For instance, if you believe you're smart, you will be more likely to be smart or act in a smart manner. Beliefs affect your perspective, your thoughts, your habits.

Beliefs may limit you or help you excel. See if you can change the meanings behind those <u>limiting</u> beliefs. If you're not sure if a belief is limiting, ask "is this useful?". For instance, is your belief about your life, your career, your identity useful? Or does it limit you? Can you adjust or even change that belief? Be aware of your beliefs and be objective.

Research shows that many of the beliefs which we hold true as an adult are actually formed when we are very young. In other words, most adults still 'believe' in things that were created in our minds as children.

Do you think that a child's mind was always correct, unbiased and accurate? Do you think that you were mature enough to encompass situations that would occur later in life as we face adulthood? Probably not. What if we really dug into our beliefs and examined the meanings behind them?

Beliefs are the intangible keys to making lasting shifts in our habits. Therefore, any strategies used to change habitual behaviors are much more effective when beliefs are addressed.

Affirmations and powerful questions play a big part in creating and maintaining beliefs. Directed questions help us to plant the seeds of a belief from which we can grow the life we desire.

Other people will have different beliefs about religion, politics, lifestyles and success. They may try to change yours. Do not change yours for them and do not try to change theirs. When others question or challenge your beliefs, don't get defensive but don't be a pushover. Too many people get too emotional when they perceive that their beliefs are being threatened. Respect their beliefs as they should respect yours. Listen, learn, objectively consider alternative views. Be open. It has been said that when your values are challenged and they hold, they are stronger. This can help make the world a better place, by the way.

As you mature, you will redefine your beliefs because of experience, wisdom and perspective.

Also; Habits form beliefs, beliefs form your values, values define your life. Beliefs have the power to create OR destroy. They can help you move ahead or hold you back.

Courage – [kur-**ij**] – the quality of mind or spirit that enables a person to face difficulty, danger, pain, etc., without fear; bravery.

Your time is limited, so don't waste it living someone else's life. Don't be trapped by dogma – which is living with the results of other people's thinking. Don't let the noise of others' opinions drown out your own inner voice. And most important, have the courage to follow your heart and intuition.-**Steve Jobs**

—

I learned that courage was not the absence of fear, but the triumph over it. The brave man is not he who does not feel afraid, but he who conquers that fear.-**Nelson Mandela**

—

Courage is what it takes to stand up and speak; courage is also what it takes to sit down and listen.-**Winston Churchill**

WORD TO LIVE BY:

Courage – I believe that courage means that you do something even though you're scared. Everyone is scared or nervous in some way. Facing fears is what makes you grow, and it's what makes heroes. Simply put, courage is when you face your fear.

You can still experience fear and be afraid — and be courageous. It isn't binary.

When you're afraid, have faith and take a step ahead and you'll be taking a step towards courage. It could be standing up to someone in school, believing in something important, or saving someone's life. It could be a small thing in your daily life, perhaps a decision. Of course, often the hard decisions in life require courage.

I know people that say 'I'm scared, therefore I have no courage.' Again, everyone gets scared. It takes courage to move ahead and face the things we're scared of....

I believe that, while knowledge and education are necessary, action takers rule the world. Action requires courage, of course. We're all scared of failing, of rejection, of the unknown, of things outside our comfort level.

One thing that I believe some people do incorrectly is believe that they need "a bunch of courage" and to bet the farm or take one large single step. I think it is just as or more important to have courage to take small steps, incremental improvements each day. Ask yourself, "What can you do today to move ahead towards your goal or dream?" Those little things need courage too – but they add up quickly – remember momentum?

Sometimes courage is required in a single moment. Sometimes courage is required over time with patience and persistence. You can do it. Go for it. Live.

Remember, too, that the word 'encourage' means inspiring or supporting others with courage. Courage inspires others. Courage is contagious.

Like the movie *We Bought A Zoo* says; "All you need is 20 seconds of insane courage."

This chapter is dedicated to those people, those loved ones and those service men and women that have inspired courage.

Comfort zone - [**kuhm**-fert] [zohn] -a situation or position in which a person feels secure, comfortable, or in control:
—

As you move outside of your comfort zone, what was once the unknown and frightening becomes your new normal. Robin S. Sharma
—

Move out of your comfort zone. You can only grow if you are willing to feel awkward and uncomfortable when you try something new. Brian Tracy
—

Life begins at the end of your comfort zone. Neale Donald Walsch
—

WORD TO LIVE BY:

Comfort Zone – to be the person we want to be, we must get out of the comfort zone.

When we lift weights, exercise, or physically exert ourselves, we may become uncomfortable in some way, but that is how we grow our muscles and improve. To get in better shape, we need to build on what we've already done. We need to stretch the muscle and grow.

When we exercise, the next time that muscle will be stronger/ better/improved.

Similarly, in life, we have to stretch our mind, our courage, ourselves.

We must become uncomfortable, we must step out of the comfort zone, take a chance, be willing to fail or make a mistake – all in order to grow. It is about progress, not perfection

It is easy to become complacent, become "busy", to find excuses or distractions and stay where we are. We can still be fun, smart, lovable, etc. in our comfort zone – but soon we'll find that we may not be growing.

The more often you move outside your comfort zone, the more comfortable you will get with uncertainty.

We all have so much incredible potential on the inside. We all have gifts and talents that we don't know anything about because we haven't seen them – they haven't come out yet. Often in moments of 'discomfort' we see different sides of us, we meet new and different people and we encounter new and different situations – all interesting and delightful. I believe to move towards self-actualization, we need to go outside our comfort zone.

I challenge you to go outside your comfort zone today.

Ego - [**ee**-goh **eg**-oh] -the part of the psychic apparatus that experiences andreacts to the outside world and thus mediates between the primitivedrives of the id and the demands of the social and physicalenvironment. Also; conceit; self-importance:

—

We must go beyond the constant clamor of ego, beyond the tools of logic and reason, to the still, calm place within us: the realm of the soul.-**Deepak Chopra**

—

Ego stops you from getting things done and getting people to work with you. That's why I firmly believe that ego and success are not compatible.-**Harvey Mackay**

—

Because of its phantom nature, and despite elaborate defense mechanisms, the ego is very vulnerable and insecure, and it sees itself as constantly under threat. This, by the way, is the case even if the ego is outwardly very confident.-**Eckhart Tolle**

—

WORD TO LIVE BY:

Ego – The ego is something that we all struggle with, especially when we're young or immature. We may think that we are better than we are, we think that we alone make things happen and that we don't need help. As we mature we realize that almost everything we have or that we achieve is because of the love, help and support of others. We realize that the ego gets in our way and that if we let our true-self go, and if we live in the moment, we will succeed, connect and enjoy life.

The ego is only an illusion – it is not really us – but it can be a very influential illusion. There are times when we may let our identity become our ego, or vice versa, and in that moment our identity can prevent us from knowing our true self. Ego is the false idea of believing that you are what you have or what you do and this is a backwards way of assessing and living life.

The ego limits us. The ego is fragile and it provides all the noisy chatter in our heads. The ego uses only logic and reason. Those things are important but life is more than just logic and reason.

Communication - \kə-ˌmyü-nə-ˈkā-shən\ - the act or process of using words, sounds, signs, or behaviors to express or exchange information or to express your ideas, thoughts, feelings, etc., to someone else

A man's character may be learned from the adjectives which he habitually uses in conversation.-**Mark Twain**

—

Any problem, big or small, within a family, always seems to start with bad communication. Someone isn't listening.-**Emma Thompson**

—

To effectively communicate, we must realize that we are all different in the way we perceive the world and use this understanding as a guide to our communication with others.-**Tony Robbins**

—

It's not what you say, it's how you say it – **Unknown**

—

WORD TO LIVE BY:

Communication-

Recently I read in an article by Brendon Burchard that stated almost everything good that has come into your life happened because of how you communicate. On the flip side, it is also mostly true that every relationship that was ruined, every sales pitch that didn't go well, or every opportunity to influence that fell flat, all came because of the way you communicate?

Any career or vocation benefits from good communication; healthcare, sales, auto mechanic, manufacturer, artist, education, management, whatever. None of us want a surgeon that doesn't communicate (or listen) well. If your mechanic has poor communication skills, that might not work out well. Today, schools are helping students learn and improve their 'soft skills', also called emotional intelligence, as part of a necessary set of abilities that all students need as they move on to college and career.

We discount our communication skills because it is something we do every single day. Sometimes we get lazy or complacent with our communication. It doesn't matter how smart or skilled someone is, if they can't communicate effectively, it doesn't matter.

As with anything, with a lack of attention comes a lack of progress. Communication is a skill that needs ongoing attention and improvement. We can learn new things and reinforce good habits. By being aware and focused on good communication, we won't just be going through the motions, we can communicate in effective, memorable, striking ways so that we connect better with those around us.

One of the best ways to communicate better is to see the situation, issue or circumstances from the other person's point of view. If you make the message about them, from their point of view, it will carry a lot more weight. Ask 'how do they perceive this?' and 'what's really important to them now?'. Remember that emotion is a big part of communication; infuse your message with the right emotions and it will work better. Don't just communicate, communicate better.

Question - [kwes-ch*uh* n] –a matter for discussion or under discussion; a matter for investigation. to dispute; challenge; to explore, investigate, ponder

—

New Year's Day. A fresh start. A new chapter in life waiting to be written. New questions to be asked, embraced, and loved. Answers to be discovered and then lived in this transformative year of delight and self-discovery. Today carve out a quiet interlude for yourself in which to dream, pen in hand. Only dreams give birth to change.-**Sarah Ban Breathnach**

—

Did I offer peace today? Did I bring a smile to someone's face? Did I say words of healing? Did I let go of my anger and resentment? Did I forgive? Did I love? These are the real questions. I must trust that the little bit of love that I sow now will bear many fruits, here in this world and the life to come.-**Henri Nouwen**

—

Judge a man by his questions rather than his answers.-**Voltaire**
—

Word to Live By:

Questions- Powerful and perfect opportunities to help prime ourselves, our points of view, our thinking, and to open ourselves and our minds to growth

We all ask ourselves questions each and every day, all day, whether we realize it or not. They say we have up to 60,000 thoughts running through our minds each day, and many of these are questions. Are they good questions? Are they useful? Do they empower us?

When we ask "What is wrong with me?" or "What can't I be ___?" or "Why am I lazy?" or "Why do I struggle?" – these questions almost never help us. Remember, part of your brain is like a computer. It is a wonderful problem solving tool. We can ponder on a problem, sleep on it, and when we least expect it – maybe in the shower, while driving, often in some relaxed state of mind, boom - the answer pops into our conscious mind.

When you ask your unconscious something, it goes out and looks for the answer. When you ask yourself, "Why can't I " ...do something OR "Why do I struggle?" your brain will search for an answer or answers. So why don't you just ask empowering questions instead?

Many of us have heard of incantations or affirmations and some of us have used them. They can help. However, sometimes when you try to say an affirmation that you don't believe, it isn't very effective. I recall when I was young, single and broke; I used some affirmation like "I am successful." I didn't believe that I was successful and when I said it, the affirmation seemed to just make me uneasy or feel inauthentic in some way.

Therefore, if you ask the question, "Why am I successful?" your brain will work on that. You change the focus. If you can spend a few minutes each day on trying to answer the question consciously, you'll feel better and build some momentum. Maybe just one thing this week will make you feel successful, and you'll build on that.

A question is very powerful. The question "Why?" probably should be asked whenever we start anything significant. If we can ask, and at least partially answer 'Why' we're doing something, we can always go back to that thought when we face challenges.

Why's are important for relationships, charities, and long term career choices. Many people volunteer. They do it for some reason. They have a 'why' which gives them hunger and motivation to help others.

Remember; "Ask Why and the How will appear".

Also….The "how's" often don't matter. How you solve a problem will work itself out later. It is easy to get caught in the how's.

Faith - \faths, *sometimes* 'fāthz\ – firm belief in something for which there is no proof

—

Faith is taking the first step even when you don't see the whole staircase.-Martin Luther King, Jr.

—

You'll see it when you believe it.-Wayne Dyer

—

You have to believe in yourself.-Sun Tzu

—

WORD TO LIVE BY:

Faith – Faith means having confidence and trust in yourself, in someone else, or in God or a higher power.

Prepare and plan for an event, do as much as you can, then have faith that it will fall into place. Have faith that you'll be protected, that you'll be safe. Have faith that you can do it. Surrender yourself to it. No worries. It's like dropping a pebble from your hand. Let go.

What if you never did something, how can you have faith?

Here is a quick story from www.tut.com; The Universe: "You had faith when you walked as a baby. This is a good lesson because your probably had lots of enthusiasm and you didn't look back at your falls. You referenced all of your successes like crawling, grunting, yelling, dancing, climbing, chewing on your fingers – all these were successful references for you which gave you confidence and pride. You had faith in yourself and the world around you and you just kept moving ahead, taking another step, sometimes falling, always getting up. Eventually, just like you thought you would, you walked, and you ran, ...it was almost magical. So here we are many days later. Look at all of those successful references you have had from your past. Good stuff, huh? So now that you've really conquered that walking thing, what are you going to do now?"

Remember to look past your ego and tap into your inner-self and believe that you can do it. Like walking, even if you never, ever did it before, have faith that you can do it – much like if you already accomplished it- as if you already know how.

Also remember to have faith in others and in this beautiful world of ours.

Sometimes we just have to let go and have faith. When we relax and be true to ourselves we can do great things.

I have faith that you can do amazing things.

Hunger – [huhng-ger] – (n.) a strong or compelling desire or craving: (v.) to have a strong desire.

—

Wanting something is not enough. You must hunger for it. Your motivation must be absolutely compelling in order to overcome the obstacles that will invariably come your way.-Les Brown

—

Being unwanted, unloved, uncared for, forgotten by everybody, I think that is a much greater hunger, a much greater poverty than the person who has nothing to eat.-Mother Teresa

—

Leaders use the emotions of hunger and drive to compel them to where they want to go. Very simply, they defy the odds—by defying their fears, limitations, and even conventional wisdom at times as well as the cultural hypnosis that leads them to accept struggle, scarcity, hopelessness and loss as unavoidable. Willing to do everything necessary to achieve their vision, leaders have set a higher standard for what they want from their lives. They have decided to step up—to take immediate action to turn their dreams into reality-Tony Robbins

—

WORD TO LIVE BY:

Hunger- I am speaking of the hunger in our hearts; the hunger to do better, to improve something, to improve yourself, to work harder and smarter, to help others, to keep going, to keep working.

Often when we're young and broke we have a hunger to do better. Sometimes when we have some kind of success or money come along, we lose that hunger. We need to keep the hunger alive, keep working and making constant, incremental improvements – even if it is not for our own benefit – perhaps it is to help others, volunteer, teach, or contribute.

Hunger, not desperation, is not based in fear. It is the desire for something better and the commitment to take action until one reaches a result. The journey provides great experiences, knowledge and education. The result provides satisfaction, accomplishment and growth. Essentially if we don't have hunger we're not growing. If we're not growing, are we then shrinking?

We can have hunger for knowledge, creativity, money, business growth, helping others, expanding and improving relationships, and much more. This is the type of hunger keeps successful people going and growing even after they have 'reached success' in our society.

You alone define and generate your Hunger.

Bonus – an article that applies to any age "If I Were 22: Hunger Will Destroy Your Fear of Failure"

http://bit.ly/2e5x0m8

Failure- [ˈfālyər] -omission of occurrence or performance; *specifically*: a failing to perform a duty or expected action

—

Far better is it to dare mighty things, to win glorious triumphs, even though checkered by failure... than to rank with those poor spirits who neither enjoy nor suffer much, because they live in a gray twilight that knows not victory nor defeat. Theodore Roosevelt

—

It is impossible to live without failing at something, unless you live so cautiously that you might as well not have lived at all, in which case you have failed by default. J. K. Rowling

—

You make mistakes. Mistakes don't make you. Maxwell Maltz

—

WORD TO LIVE BY:

Failure- something many people take great efforts to avoid but failure is essential for growth and learning

Many people use fear of failure as an excuse for not taking actions that will move them forward. What they don't understand is that you can't succeed until you fail first.

Many of us failed when we first learned to ride a bike. We all fell down, we were bruised, skinned our knee. But we a got up and continued on until we fell off again, and ultimately we learned to ride a bike.

Falling didn't stop you from trying.

Whether realized or not, people use fear of failure as an excuse to avoid taking responsibility for their actions.

There is a myth about successful people – it is that they never fail. In reality, the truth is successful people fail a lot *more* than unsuccessful people-but they don't attach any meaning to it -Just like you didn't attach meaning to it when you fell off your bike learning to ride.

Failure is an education. If I had to raise my daughters over again, I'd do it much the same but I'd try to often ask them each day, "How did you fail today?" because I want them to push themselves, try new things, and let them know that it is OK to fail, in fact it is often good.

Everyone has failures and missteps-and it's how you handle them that matters.

Here is a quick story I recently read on horsesmouth.com by Jim Rohrbach; "In the early '80s, a young singer left an abusive household in Indiana and hitchhiked to L.A., armed only with his music and an attitude. Over the next couple of years, he spent his days crashing in a rundown apartment and his nights playing with a long string of bands that never got a big break. But unlike the legions of would-be rockers who threw in the towel, Axl Rose never wavered from exactly what he wanted. He was on a mission. "Going into Guns N' Roses, there wasn't a number two [backup plan]," says the legendary front man. "At that time I was going to make it in a band, and it was all the way or bust."

Nothing can stop a man or woman with a vision.

'Make persistence your mantra'

Many of us have heard the quote, "I have not failed." Edison famously said of his lengthy pursuit of a practical prototype. "I've just found 10,000 ways that won't work."

What is our fear?

For me, I know that, especially in the past (and even occasionally today) I was too concerned with what family, friends, peers, and teachers say about what I attempt to do.

Fear of failure is a self-fulfilling prophecy; when you say you can't do something, you're selling this idea to yourself.

My father once told me, "The measure of a person is not how well they start, but how well they finish." Anyone can start. Following through and finishing is another story altogether. It takes far more fortitude to finish something than it does to start it, especially as an entrepreneur.

Thought - [THôt] - an idea or opinion produced by thinking or occurring suddenly in the mind:

—

As a single footstep will not make a path on the earth, so a single thought will not make a pathway in the mind. To make a deep physical path, we walk again and again. To make a deep mental path, we must think over and over the kind of thoughts we wish to dominate our lives. -Henry David Thoreau

—

Man is made or unmade by himself. By the right choice he ascends. As a being of power, intelligence, and love, and the lord of his own thoughts, he holds the key to every situation. Good thoughts bear good fruit, bad thoughts bear bad fruit.-James Allen

—

What matters is to live in the present, live now, for every moment is now. It is your thoughts and acts of the moment that create your future. The outline of your future path already exists, for you created its pattern by your past. -Sai Baba

—

WORD TO LIVE BY:

Thought - Call it thoughts, psychology, self-talk, whatever – I'm referring to what goes on in each of our minds each and every day. We create reality each day from our thoughts.

"Thoughts become things." Michael Dooley

Mastering your mind, your habitual thoughts, the questions that you ask yourself, your vocabulary that you use – this is a fundamental element to living your best.

Many people have good intentions, but just can't seem to overcome the negative thought patterns that overtake them and hold them back. Many people have a desire to improve, do better – but they just don't know how or why.

Try to be aware of your thoughts. When you have a bad or negative thought, just catch yourself – don't scold yourself – just let it go and try to replace it with a good thought, a thought that will help or empower you.

The author Brendon Burchard wrote an article that discusses our thoughts and says, "people have negative recurring thoughts and feelings in their life because they are giving the negative thoughts more attention than positive ones." If you keep focusing on or about negative things, your mind will be conditioned to bring them up automatically. Brendon says that you can use this same rule and apply it to good thoughts; focus on good thoughts over a period of time, and they get sealed in the brain.

We are what we think.

—

Gratitude - [**grat**-i-tood, -tyood] - the quality or feeling of being grateful or thankful:

—

Gratitude unlocks the fullness of life. It turns what we have into enough, and more. It turns denial into acceptance, chaos to order, confusion to clarity. It can turn a meal into a feast, a house into a home, a stranger into a friend. Melody Beattie

—

Give yourself a gift of five minutes of contemplation in awe of everything you see around you. Go outside and turn your attention to the many miracles around you. This five-minute-a-day regimen of appreciation and gratitude will help you to focus your life in awe. Wayne Dyer

—

Most of us never stop to consider our blessings; rather, we spend the day only thinking about our problems. But since you have to be alive to have problems, be grateful for the opportunity to have them. Bernie Siegel

—

WORD TO LIVE BY:

Gratitude – Give thanks for everything, big and small, good and bad.

If you take just a moment to count the little things as blessings, you will make your life more abundant. There are so many things that we take for granted. We live in a free country, we have food, shelter, education, safety, we have beauty in nature and in each other, we have so many people in this world that want to help, heal, give, teach and share.

Look at your coffee cup in the morning. Someone made that, glazed it, created it so that you could enjoy the coffee. Someone took great pain to package your coffee in a secure, healthy, clean, sanitary container. People worked years to improve the freshness and flavor.

When we have what we call a 'bad day' we are often in a negative mindset or one of fear or scarcity. We are looking at, focusing on what we don't have, what we lost, what we are lacking.

It has been said that wherever there is appreciation, there will be duplication. It can be said that what we focus on expands – so if you are grateful for something, you will have more of it.

If you have gratitude for challenges and 'bad' things in life, it helps to re-frame them. An experience that we could say is 'bad' can instead be thought of as experience, education, wisdom. We learned from the situation, didn't we? We are wiser and stronger for making it through. Because of that experience, we are better people, and that's worth being grateful. Think about it, we all have things in life that we may have considered 'bad' as they were happening to us. If you instead think that life is there happening <u>for</u> us rather than <u>to</u> us, and once we gain some perspective on it, we can see that that same event may in fact be a good thing for our life. When you look at a problem like that, it is no longer a 'bad' one.

Gratitude helps us re-focus.

Tony Robbins says, "You can't be grateful and angry simultaneously. You can't be fearful and be grateful simultaneously. So gratitude is really the reset button" I like that a lot. We can't be fearful if we're grateful. We can't be angry if we're grateful. We can't feel scarcity if we have gratitude.

Bonus:

Tony Robbins has a daily gratitude ritual that I try to incorporate into my day. Read more here: http://bit.ly/2fao0AI

Grit - [grit] - firmness of character; indomitable spirit:

—

We're going to be OK because of the American people. They have more grit, determination and courage than you can imagine.-**Jill Biden**

—

Over time, grit is what separates fruitful lives from aimlessness.-**John Ortberg**

—

Heroes are never perfect, but they're brave, they're authentic, they're courageous, determined, discreet, and they've got grit. – **Wade Davis**

WORD TO LIVE BY:

Grit – the determination, persistence, courage, consistency and congruency we have when we relentelessly pursue something; when we focus, have faith, take action and keep moving even when there are challenges, hurdles, setbacks.

Grit helps us take something from an idea to reality. Grit gets us through those days when nothing seems to be going right. Grit keeps us going until we finally reach our dream or goals.

Grit keeps us going through the mundane, boring, difficult tasks that ultimately help us grow and progress.

In a TED Talk, author Angela Duckworth studied, wrote about and explained grit. In her opinion grit is essentially a drive to tirelessly work through challenges, failures, and adversity to achieve set goals. She believes that people with grit are uniquely positioned to reach higher achievements than others who lack similar stamina.

Intelligence, education, wisdom, talent, skills are all important. Without action and grit, they are basically meaningless.

– BONUS VIDEO

TED TALK: Angela Lee Duckworth explains her theory of **"grit"** as a predictor of success.

http://bit.ly/2eLRv7E

Kindness - [**kahynd**-nis] - friendly feeling; liking, giving behavior, favor

—

This is my simple religion. There is no need for temples; no need for complicated philosophy. Our own brain, our own heart is our temple; the philosophy is kindness. **– Dalai Lama**

—

Kindness in words creates confidence. Kindness in thinking creates profoundness. Kindness in giving creates love. **–Lao Tzu**

—

No act of kindness, no matter how small, is ever wasted. **–Aesop**

—

WORD TO LIVE BY:

Kindness – An act of support, giving, sharing, support, love, help, or healing.

Kindness is something few of us think about in our daily lives. We're thinking about surviving, completing things, creating, getting results, communicating, building and other such things.

Are we kind? Most of us may be courteous in some manner. We may be polite. Are we kind – do we take action and reach out? Do we give, share, contribute? Not as much as we probably think that we might.

I once heard two young adults discuss how they don't receive kindness from others – friends and strangers. They didn't talk about giving kindness – being kind to others.

Being kind is the best way to receiving kindness. Others often reciprocate in some way. Even if they don't necessarily reciprocate, it has been shown that we still feel good and we have an emotional reward when we give – and those around us observing the kind act also get that same emotional pop of kindness. The giver, the receiver and the observer all gain the good feelings of just one kind act.

Like forgiveness, volunteering, sharing, love, contribution and things of that nature, kindness is something that we think that we're just doing for someone else; actually it is something that helps us each personally and the society around us. Kindness with momentum is a wonderful thing.

What if we were all just a little more kind each day? Just a simple, note, comment, act or gift?

What one act of kindness can you do for someone?

Next time if you pause before being kind, think about what Ralph Waldo Emerson said, "You cannot do a kindness too soon, for you never know how soon it will be too late."

Suggested reading: *Have You Filled A Bucket Today*? By Carol McCloud

Also consider the article "30 Acts of Kindness that Cost $1 or Less to Perform"

BY ALEX AND OLGA KARPMAN -NOVEMBER 2, 2015, Click Here: http://bit.ly/2eMwf2K

Smile – \smī(-ə)l\ – A **smile** is a facial expression formed primarily by flexing the muscles at the sides of the mouth.

A warm smile is the universal language of kindness.-**William Arthur Ward**

We shall never know all the good that a simple smile can do.-**Mother Teresa**

Too often we underestimate the power of a touch, a smile, a kind word, a listening ear, an honest compliment, or the smallest act of caring, all of which have the potential to turn a life around.-**Leo Buscaglia**

—

WORD TO LIVE BY:

Smile –Try to smile today at any appropriate chance you get. Give a smile to a stranger, a friend, a loved one. Everyone looks better with a smile. The right smile, at the right time, wins friends and calms enemies.

A recent study found that in obituaries people often, more than any other attribute, mentioned their loved one's smile. Putting a smile on your face will boost your mood and increase your potential for long-term happiness.

A genuine smile also sends the message to others that we are likeable, trustworthy and dependable – the kind of person others want to do business with, engage in conversation, or build meaningful relationships with.

Smiling stimulates our brain's reward mechanisms in a way that even chocolate, a well-regarded pleasure-inducer, cannot match. Smiling reduces stress that your body and mind feel, almost similar to getting good sleep, according to recent studies. Smiling helps to generate more positive emotions within you.

Bonus: Ted Talk -The hidden power of smiling

http://bit.ly/2eLTGbg

Excuse - \ik-'skyüz - to try to remove blame from
—

An excuse is worse and more terrible than a lie, for an excuse is a lie guarded. Pope John Paul II

—

You'll ultimately realize that there are no excuses worth defending, ever, even if they've always been part of your life— and the joy of releasing them will resonate throughout your very being. Wayne Dyer

—

One of life's fundamental truths states, 'Ask and you shall receive.' As kids we get used to asking for things, but somehow we lose this ability in adulthood. We come up with all sorts of excuses and reasons to avoid any possibility of criticism or rejection. Jack Canfield

—

WORD TO LIVE BY: (not live by)

EXCUSES- phony reasons not to get out there and succeed.

Excuses hold us back, plain and simple. We use fear as an Excuse!

Look at all of the times, the opportunities, the 'stuff of life' that you may have missed.

Could you be better off if you were less fearful? If you had fewer excuses?

I was at a nice picnic recently and there was a group of people there talking and they were just full of fear for so many things and they were talking about many things in their lives that they just didn't want to do or "just couldn't".

At first, I got a little judgmental and thought "Tsk!", and then I stopped myself. I tried to look at them and see what I didn't like – and I saw it was also in me. We all do the same thing.

I saw how I use fear as an excuse. Recently I've had various opportunities in my career and with real estate. In the past, I had a bad real estate experience, so I chose to pass on this opportunity. Looking back, it wasn't a great decision to pass like I did – I at least needed to spend more time researching – but my fears about the past clouded my current-day decision.

- Are you using fear to hold you back, consciously or unconsciously? Be honest.
- What can you do to wipe out excuses so that you can make better decisions?
- What can you do to erase fear so that you can live your life?
- What kinds of questions can you ask yourself each day to change this habit?
- What kinds of things can you do to interrupt the pattern of fear and excuses?

In one way or another most of us have an excuse about some part of our lives. Some excuses are on the surface – those that might think about consciously or those we say and share with others. Other excuses are deep down – we may know about them or not – either way, we keep them hidden deep down and may use them to convince ourselves.

Celebrate - [**sel**-*uh*-breyt] -· to observe (adayorevent)with ceremonies of respect, festivity, or rejoicing.

Imagine that you already have "it" or that you've already accomplished "it" – then celebrate!- Wayne Dyer

—

"The more you praise and celebrate your life, the more there is in life to celebrate." — Oprah Winfrey

—

"Don't forget to CELEBRATE!!!Anchor the experience of doing something truly extraordinary with an awesome celebration."- Tony Robbins

—

WORD TO LIVE BY:

Celebrate - I think we all need to celebrate more often.

Yes, I said we. As I've mentioned before, I am naturally a low-key guy. I think part of me tries to downplay things. I notice that especially with friends, with my sisters, and relatives – those with which I grew up – when something good happens or when I'm excited about something – I try to act cool, calm, and un-excited when I tell them about it.

The other day I was excited about a project at work. I was telling a relative and I noticed that right way, I downplayed the whole thing. It came off like I was actually down about it. He tried to give me some encouragement. I was actually excited.**I needed and wanted to celebrate with him but I didn't. For some reason I held back, maybe I was embarrassed. We both would have enjoyed it and benefited. We both would have bonded. We may have made a memory. The point is that I had a reason to celebrate, someone gave me the chance, and I passed it up.**

We often have opportunities to celebrate for all sorts of reasons, large and small. We need to celebrate more.
—

Just as Wayne Dyer says "Highly realized people learn to think from the end- that is, they experience what they wish to intend before it shows up in the material form." Celebrate that car, that job, that improved relationship, that newly thinner, leaner body. Enjoy it.

I practice money coming in and I get the feeling like I'm winning the lottery. I hold my arms up like Rocky on the top of the Philly steps and I jump around. I visualize and celebrate. I enjoy it.

How would you react if you won the lottery? Got a perfect job? Had that perfect car/house/relationship/health? OK, now go ahead and practice celebrating it so that when it arrives, you'll be ready. In the meantime, you'll feel great.

I'll be honest, I don't know if it will always work, but EVERYTIME I feel really great afterwards! I'm smiling, happier, energized, and guess what? I'm now looking for good things to come, it becomes a self-fulfilling prophecy.

Celebrate what you've accomplished in your life! Too many of us don't give ourselves enough credit. Look into the past, briefly, get those good references and celebrate them. You endured hurdles and mistakes and you are now the person you are because you kept moving. Celebrate it!

Celebrate the present– your family, friends, work, life, health – even if it isn't perfect. Sure you can want to improve something but hell, if you didn't have your situation now, you wouldn't have the perspective, wisdom, and knowledge to make it better. Guess what, you can help yourself now, you can even help others, you have choices, that's great, celebrate

I know that there are some days when you don't feel like celebrating. Use Tony Robbins' method "What could I celebrate today?" (then even if you can't think of something ask Tony's question) "If I could think of something to celebrate, what would it be?"

Celebrate what you want to see more of. —Feeling happy/celebratory/abundant/whatever surpasses the money in your bank account, the report from the doctor, the whatever – and transcends what others may think of you. Genuinely feeling a certain way is possible when you detach yourself from the things you desire and then celebrating it.

Don't you think that you're more attractive to others when you're thinking celebrating rather than the "ho-hum" you? Wouldn't your career be a little different if you approached it in a 'celebrating-way' rather that complaining, whining and doing the minimum as so many people do? (not you of course)

Celebrating sends a message to others around you, even to the Universe (if you believe in such)

Celebrating brings smiles and laughter. It brings joy and happiness. Enough said.

Visualize - vis·u·al·ize [ˈviZH(o͞o)əˌlīz] – form a mental image of; imagine:

Visualizing for Beginners...For those who want convenient parking spaces, unexpected gifts, or chance encounters with cool people: First, think. Second, let go.

Visualizing for the Illuminated...For those who want a healing touch, world peace, or a new steady flow of cash, abundance, and happiness. First, think. Second, let go. The Universe/Mike Dooley
—

I believe that visualization is one of the most powerful means of achieving personal goals. Harvey Mackay
—

Make sure you visualize what you really want, not what someone else wants for you. Jerry Gillies
—

WORD TO LIVE BY:

Visualize - While visualization isn't a value like some of the Words to Live By, such as "honesty", I still know that it is a key Word to use in daily life.

For a long time I wanted to visualize more often and struggled with it. I was always concerned I wasn't doing it right and probably even held off because I thought I would 'do it wrong'. Then I read one simple passage about it in a book and realized that any visualization is helpful. So I now try to do it often in different ways.

First, let's all realize and agree about an example of 'bad' visualization: Worry. When you worry, you typically picture – or visualize – something going wrong. Well, guess what, you're reinforcing that image in your mind. You are physically creating the chemical and biological connections that could make that negative thing more likely. I read once that "worrying in like praying for bad things to happen". I think that society has taught us – especially my mother's generation and many mothers in our country – that if you don't worry, you don't care. I know so many women that feel that worrying is a necessity if you have a family. Some feel that if you don't worry, you aren't as good of a mother. I say all that is wrong.

Visualizing is a form of praying, I believe. When we pray for someone that is sick or in need of help in some way, we want them to get better or find themselves in a better situation. We often pray for help and guidance in our own lives.

Visualization is very important. Regardless if you believe in the Law of Attraction, the Secret, or anything spiritual, there is so much scientific support for it. I think that schools should teach it. If you talk with any coach or athlete at a good college program, in the Olympics, or a professional athlete, they all use visualization. Arnold Palmer, Michael Jordan, Jack Nicklaus, Tiger Woods, Arnold Schwarzenegger, Jim Carrey and entire teams of players used visualization. Olympic Swimmer Michael Phelps was taught by his coach to "play the tape" each night and morning. That meant to play the mental tape, like a video, of him swimming and winning.

So many great business people use imagery and visualization. They use it for business meetings, presentations, specific events and also for the big picture strategies.

According to vanderbuilt.edu, visualization, also called mental imagery, is defined as "experience that resembles perceptual experience, but which occurs in the absence of theappropriate stimuli for the relevant perception" (plato.stanford.edu/entries/ mental-imagery/). Whenever we imagine ourselves performing an action in the absence of physical practice, we are said to be using imagery. While most discussions of imagery focus on the visual mode, there exists other modes of experience such as auditory and kinesthetic that are just as important.

One important thing I found in this study and others is that "There is no correct way to practice mental imagery."

Scientifically, there is ample evidence that visualization can significantly enhance physical skill development and increase performance in many sports. There is even evidence that visualization of weight training can lead to significant gains in muscle mass and strength!

Neurologically, visualization invokes many of the same areas of the brain involved in the actual physical manifestation of the skill. Because of this, there are tremendous neural connections that are strengthened during visualization that are transferable to the physical domain.

Visualization helps with motivation and inspiration. Put simply, when you imagine something you then remind yourself of how good it will feel to achieve your dreams, and you become more so motivated to strive for them. This motivation allows you to take the steps needed to fulfill your dreams – and feel like fun along the way.

Visualization **burns the mental picture, images, feelings and emotions into yoursubconscious mind–** a very powerful tool. Once yoursubconscious mindlatches onto an idea, it begins to work without you. It creates the belief. Your subconscious can effortlessly lead you to your goals, if it has a belief. Beliefs rule our lives. One day we couldn't do something, the next day we could. One day we believed that we could not, the next day we believed that we could. Visualization helps us believe sooner, and helps us believe when we probably would never do so.

Meaning – [mee-nin]- the end, purpose, or significance of something

—

I have always believed, and I still believe, that whatever good or bad fortune may come our way we can always give it meaning and transform it into something of value. Hermann Hesse

—

Life takes on meaning when you become motivated, set goals and charge after them in an unstoppable manner. Les Brown

—

For the meaning of life differs from man to man, from day to day and from hour to hour. What matters, therefore, is not the meaning of life in general but rather the specific meaning of a person's life at a given moment. Viktor E. Frankl

—

WORD TO LIVE BY:

Meaning – what we 'assign' to an experience, phrase, word, or event.

Lots of things 'happen to us' in life. Illness, loss, death, pain sorrow. There are also lots of events each day that come our way, small and big; traffic, business, bills, and other responsibilities.

Events happen, things happen, how we react to these things is a big deal. The meaning we give to these things makes a difference.

Sometimes we label an event. Sometimes that's not really fair or accurate. Often we need time and perspective to look back on things in our lives. Sometimes that thing that happened seemed like a bad thing for us but after all, it turned out to be good for us.

So many times there is an experience or a situation, and we automatically label it as bad. How foolish this can be – we can learn from events, they make us stronger, we learn about life and about ourselves. So many times we give negative meaning to what someone else says or does. Maybe they say that because they're jealous or sad or lonely, or maybe even because they are worried about us. What if you re-framed what other people did or said so that it was positive/empowering/helpful? Think how much better life might be if we labeled events, things people did as good.

Put simply, it isn't the events, situations, or circumstances of our lives that shape us, but our beliefs as to what those events mean....it is the meaning we assign to the event that makes the difference.

Hero -\'hir-(,)ō\- a person who is admired for great or brave acts or fine qualities

—

A hero is someone who has given his or her life to something bigger than oneself. Joseph Campbell

—

The thing about a hero, is even when it doesn't look like there's a light at the end of the tunnel, he's going to keep digging, he's going to keep trying to do right and make up for what's gone before, just because that's who he is. Joss Whedon

—

A hero is an ordinary individual who finds the strength to persevere and endure in spite of overwhelming obstacles. Christopher Reeve

—

WORD TO LIVE BY:

Hero –Anyone can be a hero. You are probably someone's hero – or at least you can be.

I've seen my parents act like heroes on behalf of others. They got no credit or recognition in that moment but even now, many years later, people younger and older still come up to me and mention it.

There have been lots of people that have done or said things for or to me that meantso much. Simple words, actions, decisions. People did things that they didn't need to do, and typically they didn't gain anything for it. They were my hero.

In the movies, the hero often faces one big challenge and overcomes it with great drama. Often those Hollywood heroes face one big event. Everyday heroes often make choices each day, often with sacrifice to themselves, and they consistently do little things for the greater good.

Being a hero means being a leader and taking a stand. Being a hero takes work, heroes can be ridiculed, and certainly being a hero can be lonely.

Most of us see or know of a situation where we could contribute to the world and be a hero. Someof us don't have the confidence in ourselves, we're scared, and often we don't take the action. Some of us simply say, "It's not my job." Will we make a mistake? Will we look like a fool? It's easier not to be a hero. However, when you take a step forward, you'll find the strength, courage, and find a way to do it. All of ushave the strength and guidance inside us - all that we need - to be a hero anytime that we want.

I recall one time there was a group of us facing the same situation and, seemingly mostly out of anger, I made a stand and said something. It was a small thing and I really didn't think it through but it worked out. Had I thought it through, I might have been intimidated or hesitant. In any case, I didn't think that it was heroic in any way. Years later, I saw someone from that group and they told me that they thought I was quite brave for doing and saying what I did. She told me that it inspired her to take action in her own life.

We never know the power of how we can influence and inspire others. As I stated above, you may be someone's hero. Do the right thing. Make a decision. Take action. Be yourself.

I believe that all of our past failures and frustrations were actually layingthe foundation so that we can be heroes. It is your decisions and your actions, not your conditions or labels that determine whether you're a hero.

Being a hero actually means being a servant to something bigger than one's self, and focusing on the greater good, as opposed to just your needs, will reap massive rewards. I think that it's important to recognize the everyday heroes and equally important to strive to be a hero.

—

BONUS:–CNN's Real everyday heroes!

http://cnn.it/1GUvGZm

Humor – [hyoo-mer*or, often,*yoo-]– a comic, absurd, or incongruous quality causing amusement:

Laughter – [laf-ter,lahf-] an inner quality, mood, disposition, etc., suggestive of laughter; mirthfulness:

I don't like country music, but I don't mean to denigrate those who do. And for the people who like country music, denigrate means 'put down'. Bob Newhart

—

I went to a bookstore and asked the saleswoman, 'Where's the self-help section?' She said if she told me, it would defeat the purpose. George Carlin

—

My friends tell me I have an intimacy problem. But they don't really know me. Garry Shandling

—

WORDS TO LIVE BY:

Humor/Laughter - You must have a sense of humor in life. (Some say God sure does.)

Life is better, easier, funnier with a sense of humor.

I'm reminded of two quotes, both anonymous: "A sense of humor always made me laugh." And "I smile more when I laugh."

Laughter releases stress. It releases endorphins and other 'good natural stuff'. Laughter immediately relaxes us and gives us a different perspective.

Humor is a great ice-breaker. We can approach controversial subjects. Humor reduces hostility, deflects criticism, improves morale, relieve tension. Humor helps us communicate difficult thoughts. Humor helps us point out the ridiculous, unjust, prejudice, and pain.

—

(Dedicated to my parents, Jim and Joan, who put humor and laughter in my life.)

Useful –[ˈyo͞osfəl] – being of use or service; serving some purpose; advantageous, helpful, or of good effect:

A life spent making mistakes is not only more honorable, but more useful than a life spent doing nothing.-**George Bernard Shaw**

—

Always desire to learn something useful.-**Sophocles**

—

We should not look back unless it is to derive useful lessons from past errors, and for the purpose of profiting by dearly bought experience.-**George Washington**

—

WORD TO LIVE BY:

Useful – Ask a simple question, "Is this useful?"

We all do many things, we have beliefs, and we've had habits that we have done for years.

Maybe we're scared of something and we've been scared for a long time.

Maybe it is a more recent belief.

For instance, someone might say, "I am scared of flying. Therefore I rarely fly. I avoid flying."

Ask this: "IS IT USEFUL?"

By not flying, does it negatively affect my life? Who is losing out on something because of my fear? Family? Experiences? Maybe my children won't experience something, I won't build a relationship, I won't meet someone, see something, broaden something – you don't know what you don't know.

We can change our beliefs. Being scared to fly isn't useful. Change the belief.

OR, maybe we have a daily habit. Something we do each day.

Ask this: "IS IT USEFUL?"

For example: We get worried or anxious every morning before arriving at work. Is it useful? Does it help? Probably not ever…. (I believe that your state of mind is everything!)

We may already know worry doesn't help but asking the question makes us aware, perhaps in a different way, and we can address the issue differently.

Some people like to always be in control.**Ask this: "IS IT USEFUL?"**

How does it affect others? Can you let go and have faith? Letting go lets us act more naturally, more inspired, closer to God even, perhaps. Being in control also takes away the chance for others to lead or be independent.

Other things? Drinking soda? Eating sweets? Not Exercising? Being right in an argument? Making sure you get the last word? Being in charge? **Are these all useful?**

Lastly, how about that self-talk we all do?
You say thousands of things to yourself each day.

You have thoughts, images, mini-movies playing all day, everyday.

You ask yourself many questions each day.

Catch yourself next time later today and tomorrow and be aware of the thoughts.

Ask this: "IS IT USEFUL?"

We often make it harder on ourselves don't we?

Habits, beliefs, thoughts, actions.....

Asking the question "Is it useful?" can help us be more aware, which helps us correct and adjust things, if we desire it.

Worry:[wur-ee, wuhr-ee] – to torment oneself with or suffer from disturbing thoughts; fret.

Worry never robs tomorrow of its sorrow, it only saps today of its joy.-Leo Buscaglia

—

A day of worry is more exhausting than a week of work.-John Lubbock

—

I think my mother... made it clear that you have to live life by your own terms and you have to not worry about what other people think and you have to have the courage to do the unexpected.-Caroline Kennedy

—

WORD TO (not) LIVE BY:

Worry:[wur-ee, wuhr-ee] – to torment oneself with or suffer from disturbing thoughts; fret.

—

Worrying is a learned habit. (It can be unlearned) Worrying is almost always useless. It has been said that worrying is like praying for bad things to happen. Worrying makes us feel worse, it makes us focus on things we don't want, it makes us tense and unhappy, it takes us away from what we do want or hope for.

We can interrupt the pattern of worrying anytime we want. We can choose to think of good things, hope for good outcomes, or even simply stop worrying and take action instead!

Just catch yourself next time worrying – it's ok, don't punish yourself – just stop, breathe, and be in the present. Notice things around you. Feel the breeze. Listen to your breath. You can't be in the moment and worry.

—

In our society, sometimes some of us think that worrying shows love or caring for another. Traditionally our grandmothers and mothers would say something like, "I worry about you" and maybe they sometimes mean, "I care about you." We can care about someone or love them without worrying about them.

—

Instead of worrying, think about good things for our loved ones. Instead of worrying, write a list of things you're grateful for, happy about, hopeful for, action steps – or just go take action.

Write someone a quick positive letter instead of worrying. Send out some good energy!

—

I've heard someone say that 'Worry makes us immobilized in the present moment as a result of things that may or may not happen in the future, or things that have already happened and we can't change.' So why do it? Does it help? No! Is it useful, no.

—

—

BONUS Article:

Worried? How Not to Let It Get the Best of You

Read more: http://bit.ly/2epwfHV

Response – [ri-spons] – an answer or reply, as in words or in some action.

Reaction – [ree-ak-shuh n] – action in response to some influence, event, etc.:

How people treat you is their karma; how you react is yours.-Wayne Dyer

—

It's not what happens to you, but how you react to it that matters.-Epictetus

—

Failure happens all the time. It happens every day in practice. What makes you better is how you react to it.-Mia Hamm

—

WORDS TO LIVE BY

Response/Reaction – When something happens, what we do next.

How we respond is everything.

I've heard two men speak from the same deadly, gruesome battle in Vietnam describe and react differently. Both were from the same group. Both saw many people around them die. Both were woumded. Both endured the same things, yet they responded, reacted, described and thought about the battles differently.

One thought that people are inherently evil or violent and that the battle scarred him forever. He saw the deaths as losses and still felt wounded decades later. The other man saw that life was a precious gift, that he had a second chance, that he cherished the friendships and memories of those men that perished, and he felt the same way for those people that have been in his life since. Consequently, their lives since then have been much different.

We all react to small daily situations and big life decisions in our own way. We can change our ways. When you face a challenge, hit a wall, or experience failure, what do you do next? What do you believe about it? What questions do you ask? Is it time to just give up? Or do you keep going? Do you believe that the experience was an education or just a waste of time?

How do you react to loved ones and co-workers? Do you think of their point of view? Are you selfish? Are you aware of yourself, others, and situations?

—

How do you respond? We all face challenges. What you do next is what really counts.

Learning - ['lərniNG]- knowledge acquired through experience, study, or being taught:

—

He who is not everyday conquering some fear has not learned the secret of life.-**Ralph Waldo Emerson**

—

I am always ready to learn although I do not always like being taught.-**Winston Churchill**

Live as if you were to die tomorrow. Learn as if you were to live forever.-**Mahatma Gandhi**

WORD TO LIVE BY:

Learning – Never stop learning.

In my opinion, there is no end to education. There should not be a point in time that one can say, "OK, I'm done".

It is not that you read a book, pass an examination, and finish with learning.

All of life, from the moment you are born to the moment you die, is a process of learning. We should constantly search or fresh new ideas. We need to constantly sharpen our knowledge. Learning and improving our minds must be ongoing.

Sometimes the best way to learn something well is to teach it.
Often those who listen well, learn more.
Those who learn constantly often have an open-mind.
Those who ask questions learn more.

Learning keeps our mind young and active.
Knowledge can be acquired and skill-sets developed anywhere –
learning is unavoidable and happens all the time. However, lifelong
learning is about creating and maintaining a positive attitude to
learning both for personal and professional development.

Lifelong learners are motivated to learn and develop because
they want to: it is a deliberate and voluntary act.

Lifelong learning can enhance our understanding of the world
around us, provide us with more and better opportunities and
improve our quality of life.

Certainty-cer·tain·ty-[ˈsərtntē] –firm conviction that something
is the case:

—

In order to accomplish anything, we need a sense of certainty.
Our references help us to build this important emotional state.
However, if we have no experience in doing something, how
can we be certain about it? Realize you're not limited to your
actual experience: your imagination has unlimited references
to support you.–**Tony Robbins**

—

You should have certainty in what you do. 'Faith' and 'trust' are
words that put the power in the hands of an outside force that we

are meant to rely on – whether it is God or a person or the universe. Certainty puts the power back in our hands.-**Yehuda Berg**

—

If you develop the absolute sense of certainty that powerful beliefs provide, then you can get yourself to accomplish virtually anything, including those things that other people are certain are impossible.-**William Lyon Phelps**

WORD TO LIVE BY:

Certainty- Do you recall the last time that you were certain about something….and you knew it was right, and you were right? Maybe it was at work, maybe it was with your family or a relationship – for each of us it is different – it may have come from your head, or maybe your heart…..but you felt CERTAIN.

When you meet someone that is certain, you can tell it. Often the person that is most certain is most influential in the situation. Certainty is much like confidence. It comes across in someone's way of acting, their attitude and words.

Think about a situation where you felt certain. Picture it in your mind. How did you feel? Now, feel how you did when you were certain. Stand up. Get into that moment…….feel certain. ….really certain. There is a calmness, coolness about it perhaps? You feel confident. You probably feel relaxed – although energized too. What is your posture and physiology like?

Stand as if you were certain! Are your shoulders sagging or are you standing tall? How is your breathing?

Now stand as if you are Absolutely Certain! How would you stand? Breathe? What is your posture, your physiology? What is your appearance? How are you talking? How are you holding your head?

Certainty is achieved from our posture, physiology, and attitude….. your state of mind, your state of your body. You own the situation. You own the moment.

Tony Robbins has a list of what he calls the SIX HUMAN NEEDS. Certainty/Comfort, Variety, Significance, Connection/Love, Growth, and Contribution. Tony discusses Certainty this way– We all want comfort and much of this comfort comes from certainty. Of course there is no ABSOLUTE certainty, but we want certainty the car will start, the water will flow from the tap when we turn it on and the currency we use will hold its value. We search for certainty in other parts of our life. At one time there appeared to be certainty in some industries and jobs.

Sometimes I find certainty in other ways…..I don't know who told me once but they told me 'Nothing in life is permanent, no problem is permanent,it is passing; your Soul is permanent. You are permanent. Nothing is so inescapablethat you can't move on…."

Knowing that 'this too shall pass' helps me 'shake off' something bad and I feel a little relieved, calmer, and more certain. Look at the big picture. Look at other –other people have recovered from this and worse.I also think about the good things in my life. I focus on what is working and I feel more certain. I look back in my life and recall how I overcame other challenges,

I look at my successes, I look at my loved ones and support network. We are not alone. I personally believe in a Creator that is benevolent. I don't pretend to understand or label but I believe in something.

We all have this power, this source, this strength inside of each of us. We've all felt it from time to time in our lives. It often feels like the 'real person', the person at the core of ourselves. When we access this part of us, we operate from a foundation of certainty, don't we? But it does take a moment for each of us to access it – being calm, focused, even meditation….. the point is that YOU can access the certainty inside. You can reach in and grab it – **you don't have to look outside.**

Extraordinary people bring certainty into uncertain environments. Whether it be in sports, business, or even being a great parent, in times of uncertainty people are drawn to those who've somehow found a way to find an internal certainty that can guide them. That certainty is not that you have all the answers, but rather that there's certainty inside you that, together with your loved ones, you can find the answer and move forward.

Lastly, having a Vision in mind is also key. If you have that END IN MIND – the dream, the vision of what you want, if you spend time visualizing it and really feeling it – feeling as if it is already happening NOW, then you will be able to access certainty. If you know where you're going and you know that you're not going to give up until you get there, then it's OK when you encounter big and little challenges in life. You're certain that you'll reach the end and you're certain things are working out. The path may be not as you expected but no path it.

Focus on asking the right questions to yourself and focus on what you say to yourself. Are your words and self-talk building up or breaking down certainty in you?

Like you, I've had successes and also been in tough jambs. There were times when I thought my life was over financially and I was embarrassed, stressed, whatever. But as I look back, in the big picture, that was just part of the journey. Those things passed. Other things will pass, I am certain of it! My real friends are still around. That 'real Jim' is still inside me. Struggles bring strength. Strength brings certainty.

Why – [hwahy, wahy]– for what? for what reason, cause, or purpose?:
—

When you're surrounded by people who share a passionate commitment around a common purpose, when they know their 'why', anything is possible.-Howard Schultz
—

Before you start some work, always ask yourself three questions – Why am I doing it, What the results might be and Will I be successful. Only when you think deeply and find satisfactory answers to these questions, go ahead.-Chanakya
—

He who has a why to live can bear almost any how.-Friedrich Nietzsche
—

WORD TO LIVE BY:

Why – Asking ourselves why we're doing something, saying something, asking what is our purpose in the moment or overall.

The word Why is powerful for two main reasons:

First, by asking the correct "Why?" question, we can either help our brains help us, or the opposite. For instance, we all have self-talk. We all ask ourselves questions inside like: why am I so unlucky? Why do bad things happen to me? Why or what is wrong with me? Etc.......These questions will send your brain (which acts very much like a computer) on a mission to answer the question, and it will come back with an answer.

Therefore if you say, why will I never be rich?, your brain will search and find reasons why you won't be and essentially reinforce your negativity – a self-fulfilling prophecy. Yet if you interrupt your pattern and change the question to "why am I finally saving for a fun, strong financial future?" (or whatever) your brain will search for those answers.

Ask "why am I so happy", "why am I confident"…and try to answer it consciously and also let your brain answer unconsciously. It is almost magical how it works. "Why do I get so many good referrals?" or "why do I have so many good, fun, supportive friends?" is a lot better than "why don't I have any business?" or "why are most people mean?", etc. It changes your perspective, opens you to new thinking and seems to have the ability to make big changes, trust me.

Second,Why is wonderful for establishing purpose – why are you doing something? This can be for your whole life–Why are you here? It could be for a specific project-Why do I want to do a great job and get this done by October 31? Or maybe it is how you inspire others and lead a group of some kind.

Establish the "Why" and the how and what will work out. Establish the "Why" and the motivation will come more easily. Why helps us with ethical decisions, changes in life circumstances, and any challenge.

Some organizations and some leaders ask the question "why?" and they are then able to inspire where others aren't. As the below referenced TED Talk suggests, every person, every organization knows what they do. Some know how they do it, whether you call it your differentiated value proposition or your proprietary process or your USP.

Very few people or organizations know why they do what they do. To clarify, when I say this, by "why," I mean: What's your purpose? What's the cause? What's your belief? Why does your organization exist?

Why do you get out of bed in the morning? And why should anyone care?

As a result, the way we think, we act, the way we communicate is from the outside in, it's obvious. We go from the clearest thing to the fuzziest thing.

If you want to live an inspired life, if you want to be an inspired leader and or part of an inspired organization—one must think, act and communicate from the inside out....whether on a personal level or organizational level.

So, first, when you're talking to yourself, make sure you ask empowering, positive "Why?" questions.

Then, when you embark on a project, think about life, inspire others, or just want to do the best job that you can do, ask yourself "Why?" and define your purpose.

Fear-['fir]- an unpleasant emotion caused by the belief that someone or something is dangerous, likely to cause pain, or a threat:

—

I love the man that can smile in trouble, that can gather strength from distress, and grow brave by reflection. 'Tis the business of little minds to shrink, but he whose heart is firm, and whose conscience approves his conduct, will pursue his principles unto death.-**Thomas Paine**

—

I have learned over the years that when one's mind is made up, this diminishes fear; knowing what must be done does away with fear.-**Rosa Parks**

—

Everyone gets scared, everyone has fear. It's what you do next that counts. It's how you overcome the fear, or use it, that sets you apart. –**L. James Frey**

—

WORD TO LIVE BY:

Fear – A normal feeling that everyone has. Use it to remind you to be alert and aware. Do not let fear stop you or hinder you. Courage means only that you continue to move ahead, not that fear is absent.

I heard a relative of mine talking the other day about her fear. She said that she could never be courageous because she has a lot of fear.

First, I thought that the conversation and state of mind probably wasn't empowering to anyone.

Second, I tried to relate to her that courage is actually not the absence of fear but working through fears, overcoming fear- or at least trying to overcome it. I've read and seen many people labeled 'brave' state that they did in fact feel fear but went ahead anyway and did that thing.

I believe that each time we face our fears we become stronger, we learn more, we gain confidence, we build a mental muscle so that next time we can more easily face our fears.

When we are in a fearful state, it can be said that we are at our most primitive and basic state. Our 'reptile mind' then takes over. With fear we can't hear ourselves; our own voice. We may not be able to hear the beliefs and convictions that we hold to be true.

Encouragement – [en-**kur**-ij-m*uh* nt, -**kuhr**-]: help, support
—

The finest gift you can give anyone is encouragement. Yet, almost no one gets the encouragement they need to grow to their full potential. If everyone received the encouragement they need to grow, the genius in most everyone would blossom and the world would produce abundance beyond the wildest dreams. We would have more than one Einstein, Edison, Schweitzer, Mother Theresa, Dr. Salk and other great minds in a century. Sidney Madwed

—

Peer pressure works in both directions. Do we encourage? Do we support? Do we set a good example? Tony Dungy

—

Life can be tough, it can offer challenge. We can lift each other up, we can tear down, or we can do neither, just passing through life without input or gusto. We all need encouragement. We need support. Humans need this sort of thing from our friends and from strangers.- Unknown

—

WORD TO LIVE BY:

Encouragement – To share or bring spirit to or with others. To help lift up, to lead, to help each of us remember what gifts that we really have.

Years ago, I was unemployed for the first time in my life and I struggled to find a new job. Frankly, it seemed that I applied everywhere and I would have taken just about anything. The recession/Lehman Bros. "thing" happened and I just was in a funk anyway, so it was tough. I finally did find a good job at a solid company. I had a boss that was very encouraging and very supportive. Many people on the team were also encouraging, helpful, etc.

I had a tough time getting out of my own 'funk' and getting back the confidence and esteem that I once had. Part of the job required me to go away for training with others from around the country. I really enjoyed the whole experience and think about those people and times fondly. I recall that first day at training. We were all pushed outside of our comfort zone, which was good but hard. I knew no one. I was struggling to do well.... we all had to do a few different tasks, presentations, calls, proposals, etc. etc.

Then, one of the other 'students' just like me, made a comment. I wish I could remember exactly what he said. I think that I was just plain shocked, I wasn't expecting it. Anyways, he encouraged me that I did some things well. He stated how he had struggled with the same thing and was right there with me.

He didn't gain anything by helping or encouraging me – at least none that I could see. He was just being a good guy. Others in our group continued to encourage each other. I found myself doing it more than usual. We became a cohesive group and stayed in touch for quite a long time after, which was unusual, I'm told.

I think back in grade school, in high school, college, and in life. Sometimes, like the example above, I don't remember what someone said specifically, but I definitely recall times when people offered encouragement. It may have been something small like spelling a word, hitting a ball, doing a chore. It sometimes was regarding bigger things like a relationship, a job, a big financial challenge. I can still see and feel those words of encouragement. They still warm my heart today.

I think about times when I encouraged others. First, it feels good to me when I think about supporting others. Second, I frankly am a little sad that I don't recall doing it more often. I know that going forward, I want to do it more in the present and future. It isn't that hard, is it? Encouragement, support, help isn't that hard.

Real friends are loving in an unconditional manner. They accept you for your faults, the quirky things that you do or so, and regardless of what you "do for them." Friends offer support. Friends are a good influence. Friends offer encouragement. We need to choose our friends carefully. It doesn't matter their income, status, style, or dress.

Do we provide a positive influence to others? Are we complainers? Do we point out others weaknesses or kick them while we are down? Or do we help them up and give them a gentle push when they need it?

Encouraging others is about helping them focus on what they're doing right, what's going right in their life, and what good things they have to offer. We can encourage others by helping them see the donut and not the hole. We can be positive. Encouragement might include specific words like "you can do it." Sometimes it might be a silent action of setting an example. Sometimes it is simply a sign of solidarity.

I believe that we are each created for a reason, that we have a purpose. It may be something big and cool like writing a bestseller, saving a life, or something spectacular. Or it may be simply giving that one person, maybe even a stranger, that little bit of encouragement one day in our life. Maybe it's about that one little comment that we gave our friend, which seemed almost inconsequential to us, that literally saved their life as they were going through their challenges.

I recall a tough time when many people around me seemed to question me, put me down, and I questioned myself, I made some bad choices and I was feeling low. Then I happened to think about two little statements – one statement my father said to me once about his own struggles and basically amounted to being "if I can do it Jim, then you certainly can do it….". Another one was from a teacher of mine….I'm sure he made the comment almost in passing and probably forgot about it soon after, but his words of encouragement have helped me keep moving on for years and I even thought about it again this morning when I had something come up.

There are studies that show that when we encourage, support or help others, it not only helps that person's spirit, mind and body, we the encourager benefit. Endorphins and other good things flow in our bodies and theirs – we both feel good. But wait, it's not over yet – studies also show that observers, people who watch you and I encourage another person – also benefit – they have many of the same 'feel good' benefits. All three parties win. We all receive the benefit of encouragement.

There is an article titled "19 Healthy Reasons to Help Others" from the Huffington Post that states**"If you see someone who is drowning and throw him a rope, he gets a benefit, no question** about it. But you might, too. Your body might flood with feel-good chemicals that have a deep evolutionary heritage. You might get a little extra buffer from life's stresses. Your heart might beat a little healthier. Your immune system might perk up. Your mood might lift."

There is a great book for children – but we all can benefit from reading it – about helping others. *Have You Filled a Bucket Today: A Guide to Daily Happiness for Kids….* by Carol McCloud -except it should just say "for people".

As I mentioned above, sometimes I just don't think about encouraging others as much as I should, or as I'd like to ….. but I certainly want to ….. I'd love to provide a positive influence on others each and everyday.

When was the last time you made a call, wrote a letter, said something along the lines of encouragement? Can you mentor someone? Is there even something little or anonymous that you can do?

Encouraging others leaves a wonderful trail of great memories in our lives and the lives of others. Like the memories I spoke of above from loved ones and from strangers, these memories will hang around for years and for decades. Let's create some encouraging memories, let's create some goodwill and do unto others what we'd like done to us.

I can't recall where I heard it or who said it but I paraphrase this to you, 'When the need for encouragement words or inspirational words come, it does not matter who is saying them or why but what becomes vital is to feel encouraged, motivated and inspired to take whatever life throws as you.'

No matter where you are in life or what your consequences are, you can give….and I bet when you give, you'll receive something back too.

What can you do to encourage yourself? Ask great questions – empowering questions. Think about past successes, reflect on good things in life, talk nicely to yourself.

What can you do otherwise? Do you know of an encouraging book? Watch a good movie (like Rocky perhaps)?

What are some encouraging songs and music that can kick start your day?

What are some ways that you can encourage yourself in the morning? In the car?

What people in your life encourage you? Did you thank them?Can you return the favor? Can you emulate them to help others? How can you build habits around encouragement?

Can you challenge someone? Can you mentor? Can you just lend support?

—

The word Encouragement has meaning- to put in the heart -the prefix "en" which means "to put into" and the Latin word "cor" which means heart. What can you do to help others "to take heart" when the going gets tough?

If an encouraging thought comes to mind, share it, When you introduce someone, add a few words of praise, Write someone a note, Be present in the moment with them.

> *I challenge you to make your life a masterpiece.*
> *I challenge you to join the ranks of those people*
> *who live what they teach, who walk their talk.*
> — *Tony Robbins*

Bonus: Another great article about how volunteering may help your health: http://bit.ly/2epymeG

Friendship -[frend-**ship**] - a relationship between two people who hold mutual affection for each other.[1]Friendships and acquaintanceship are thought of as spanning across the same continuum.

—

No love, no friendship, can cross the path of our destiny without leaving some mark on it forever. Francois Mauriac

—

You'll make more friends in two weeks if you genuinely show interest in them than you'll have in two years if you try to get them interested in you. Dale Carnegie

—

You are the average of the 5 people you spend the most time with. Jim Rohn

—

WORD TO LIVE BY:

Friendship is a big subject to talk about. Sure, we know that friendship can be great, fun, supportive, healthy, and all that stuff.

The above definition certainly is accurate, yet probably quite general and somewhat irrelevant. For many of us, we might sometimes view friendship as just people we "hang" with – people we party with – or just people we know.

Sometimes I think that the masses of society may get caught in the frame of mind what we 'get out of' a friendship, status, popularity and so on. On the other hand, my parents told me to choose friends, not because they are popular, attractive, rich, athletic, etc – but because they are good people and because you enjoy them – and that they can lift you up.I know that I need to focus on being a better friend.

Do you lift up your friends? Do you encourage them? I like to think that I do but I confess that I probably don't as much as I'd like to…we get caught up in our own problems and lives and make excuses. We need to lead, to help friends by example. We need to lift them up with sincere words of encouragement. Life can be challenging enough, friends shouldn't bring us down with complaining and negativity.

My parents would comment on my friends really only in oneway – not how they dressed or where they lived – but how they might raise me up or encourage me. My parents were frank when they saw a friend bringing me down, belittling me – or even one that was sad or depressed all the time. They let me make my own decisions but I am grateful that I was able to see the difference between the blamers/complainers and those people who help you stay positive, laugh and make good decisions.

Are your friends bringing you down? Lifting you up? Do you lift up your friends?

Values are a big part of friendship. If we don't share values with our friends, often we no longer stay friends. We definitely should be *friendly* but maybe at some point our friendship doesn't go deeper?

I am a part of a few charities. Not a lot but it's nice. There are people there from all walks of life and income. However in most cases, we're all a like because we give our time or efforts in some way, and we're concerned for that specifc purpose or mission in some way.

NFL coach and player Tony Dungy speaking on friendship, values, and experiences with charities once said, "What matters is the reinforcement and reminders that these men bring to me that affect so many areas of my life. We may not share the same way of doing things but we share the same values."

My children went to a private school and the tuition does limit our personal funds from time to time but we know that many parents there share our values, our commitment and because of that, we have made wonderful friends.

You may have a long list of friends but how long is the list of those people you talk to or with when life's big decisions come along? Who do you seek for wisdom, laughter, insight and stability? Who stands by you? Who puts their interests before your own? Even if you disagree, talking about decisions and life's challenges with a friend is priceless, especially in lieu of listening to the voices of the crowd and society. Are you on their 'short list'?

Here's a few friendship stories...

I have a good friend from grade school. We lost contact then regained it years ago and we've been very close. Ironically we are very similar in many ways yet very different in others.Through most of our lives we have often beenphysically sized the same and have some of the same attributes. I think that we have similar values regarding our family. He thinks aboutcareer and workdifferently in some ways and in his career he focuses on one thing with great diligence. Our personalities are different.I say this as a compliment, as I often can get distracted and I could move from one field to the next. He has been there as a friend for years. We're definitely not sentimental or sappy with each other. We've seen each at our worst and best moments. In some ways we've told each other about it, too. When things got tough, he was a guy that was always supportive and easy to hang with, allowing me to joke, laugh, and enjoy life. It is tough for me tothink of one specific thing he has done or said but I do know that as a friend, he has continued to support me and be a great guy.

In college, there was a small group of us that started to hang out, mostly due to the geography of our dorm rooms. We are from different backgroundsyet we clicked. Today we all have different lives but many of us still stay in touch. We like to joke and enjoy life. We are supportive of each other. We've seen each at our worst and best moments. Often we have been able to talk with each other about all sorts of challenges that life offers. When I lost family members, lost my job, and had other financial issues, these few guys were there. In some ways we might not talk for over a month, but then when we do, we re-connect and we're there. I guess more recently I've felt like I have less to give these guys but hopefully I've been there for them when they needed it.

There are a fewpeople that are also parents of my children's classmates. Because of our kids, we hang out together. I've been very fortunate that many of thesemen and womenare greatpeople. Again, many of them have seen each us at our worst and best moments during times of loss and weakness. Like our other friends, we've celebrated events and had fun together. We've created great memories with these friends and our kids. We share laughter and fun.

There are other friends, too numerous to mention. I have afriend, an older buddy and mentor, who has been a great supporter, like an uncle of sorts; I've had bosses and managers close to my age who I still feel are friends and mentors. I've been lucky to have mentors of different kinds and different ages; these people have believed in me, sometimes more than I did in myself, and they gave me opportunities where I could excel. They helped me in these opportunities as well; often selflessly.

As I write this I find it difficult to describe all those things that are part of my friendships. There is laughter, communication, sharing ideas, support, venting, bouncing ideas, companionship, new experiences, shared experiences, and help. There is confidence, encouragement, guidance, and feedback. There are prayers, best wishes and caring thoughts.

There is ribbing, laughter, jokes, and things that snap us back to reality.

It's nice when you can talk with someone about almost anything and not be judged. It's great to know that, if you really needed it, a friend would be there with financial support if times really were pressing. Friends help us build memories and they enrich our lives. We help each other and we both benefit from these efforts.

Again, I come back to humor, laughter and happiness – what else is there really? We need to learn to laugh more at ourselves; friends help us stay lose and to keep our perspective in check when we start complaining about life. Friends challenge us by words or by example. Friends drop everything to come to your aid. Friends comforting each other during times of loss is so very powerful and meaningful.

Friendship, at least those that I've known, is about giving. So many people have been kind to me, being helpful, sharing, supportive – with no expectation of anything in return. They did it because we were friends or because it was right – or both.

As my daughters grow, I see that they have all sorts (and sources) of friends, and I'm happy about that. They don't judge their friends even though they've had friends from different economic and social backgrounds, which is great. They've had friends help them through losses and tough times, and vice versa. I am comforted to know that they are great friends to others as well. Regardless of our wallets and our status.

Recently, my wife and I had a medley of friends over and we're so lucky, and so grateful for all the people in our lives. I know it sounds corny in many ways but I can't imagine facing the challenges we've faced without friends. Sometimes just knowing that there is someone 'there' is enough.

Hey, what are friends for?

Risk - [risk] exposure to the chance of injury or loss;

—

Only those who will risk going too far can possibly find out how far one can go. T. S. Eliot

—

There are 30,000 days in your life. When I was 24, I realized I'm almost 9,000 days down. There are no warm-ups, no practice rounds, no reset buttons. Your biggest risk isn't failing, it's getting too comfortable. Every day, we're writing a few more words of a story. I wanted my story to be an adventure and that's made all the difference. Drew Houston

—

We must have courage to bet on our ideas, to take the calculated risk, and to act. Everyday living requires courage if life is to be effective and bring happiness. Maxwell Maltz

—

WORD TO LIVE BY:

Risk – we all face risks each day, some perceived, some not.

Each day many of us risk our lives hurtling our bodies and our loved ones in a potentially deadly situation, where only a thin line of paint separates us from strangers who could cause us death or severe bodily injury. We face this every day and almost never think about it, and we casually, confidently overcome it. Yes, this is driving on the road.

Think about it, we'll trust hundreds or thousands of total strangers with our lives – we trust that they will obey the rules and lines of the road and not run into us. Yet, many times we don't trust loved ones in our lives – or we don't trust ourselves to take a risk.

Risk is about how you frame it, how you perceive it.

Risk started the day you took your first breath out of the womb. Risk brings both failure and success, and certainly brings education and experience.

To change, to grow, we must take risks.

Noah St. John, author and owner of http://noahstjohn.com/writes:

3 main benefits of risk-taking:

1. You face your fear-And once you face that fear, that fear can't run your life any more.

2. *You become stronger-Once you realize that you are stronger than your fear, you often discover that you're stronger than you thought you were.*

3. *Your life changes in ways you couldn't have predicted or imagined.*

(More on this in the Bonus link below)

(Let's not get confused with a careless or reckless risk – in this case we're talking about calculated and thoughtful risks.)

What are we waiting for anyhow? This is not a rehearsal, this is the final performance. Go for it.

—

BONUS: The Benefits of Taking Risks - http://bit.ly/2nNSv24

More Quotes………

Did you like the quotes shared so far? Do you want more?

Here is a collection of MORE quotes based on those Words to Live By!

ACTION

Do you want to know who you are? Don't ask. Act! Action will delineate and define you. .-**Thomas Jefferson**

—

When it is obvious that the goals cannot be reached, don't adjust the goals, adjust the action steps. **–Confucius**

—

I never worry about action, but only inaction.-**Winston Churchill**

—

Action expresses priorities.-**Mahatma Gandhi**

—

Action is the foundational key to all success.-**Pablo Picasso**

—

A real decision is measured by the fact that you've taken a new action. If there's no action, you haven't truly decided.-**Tony Robbins**

—

An ounce of action is worth a ton of theory.-**Ralph Waldo Emerson**

—

There are risks and costs to action. But they are far less than the long range risks of comfortable inaction.-**John F. Kennedy**

—

Never confuse motion with action.-**Benjamin Franklin**

Momentum

—

When you're that successful, things have a momentum, and at a certain point you can't really tell whether you have created the momentum or it's creating you. Annie Lennox

—

Sometimes thinking too much can destroy your momentum. Tom Watson

—

One way to keep momentum going is to have constantly greater goals. Michael Korda

—

Enthusiasm is the energy and force that builds literal momentum of the human soul and mind. Bryant H. McGill

---

BELIEFS

Live your beliefs and you can turn the world around.-Henry David Thoreau

—

Frisbeetarianism is the belief that when you die, your soul goes up on the roof and gets stuck.-George Carlin

—

Believe that life is worth living and your belief will help create the fact. Belief creates the actual fact.-William James

—

One person with a belief is equal to ninety-nine who have only interests.-John Stuart Mill

—

Realizing that our actions, feelings and behavior are the result of our own images and beliefs gives us the level that psychology has always needed for changing personality.-Maxwell Maltz

—

It's the repetition of affirmations that leads to belief. And once that belief becomes a deep conviction, things begin to happen.-Muhammad Ali

COURAGE

He who is not courageous enough to take risks will accomplish nothing in life.-**Muhammad Ali**

—

You will never do anything in this world without courage. It is the greatest quality of the mind next to honor.-**Aristotle**

—

You gain strength, courage, and confidence by every experience in which you really stop to look fear in the face. You are able to say to yourself, 'I lived through this horror. I can take the next thing that comes along.-**Eleanor Roosevelt**

—

Efforts and courage are not enough without purpose and direction.-**John F. Kennedy**

—

Have the courage to say no. Have the courage to face the truth. Do the right thing because it is right. These are the magic keys to living your life with integrity.-**W. Clement Stone**

—

Don't Make Assumptions. Find the courage to ask questions and to express what you really want. Communicate with others as clearly as you can to avoid misunderstandings, sadness and drama. With just this one agreement, you can completely transform your life.-**Miguel Angel Ruiz**

—

One isn't necessarily born with courage, but one is born with potential. Without courage, we cannot practice any other virtue with consistency. We can't be kind, true, merciful, generous, or honest.-**Maya Angelou**

Comfort Zone

To the degree we're not living our dreams, our comfort zone has more control of us than we have over ourselves. Peter McWilliams

—

If you put yourself in a position where you have to stretch outside your comfort zone, then you are forced to expand your consciousness. Les Brown

—

The comfort zone is the great enemy to creativity; moving beyond it necessitates intuition, which in turn configures new perspectives and conquers fears. Dan Stevens

EGO

Let go of the ego's need to be right. When you're in the middle of an argument, ask yourself: Do I want to be right or to be happy?–**Wayne Dyer**

—

Nations have their ego, just like individuals.-**James Joyce**

—

The minute you start compromising for the sake of massaging somebody's ego, that's it, game over.-**Gordon Ramsay**

—

To walk around with an ego is a bad thing. To have confidence in yourself is a great thing.-**Fred Durst**

Communication

Effective communication is 20% what you know and 80% how you feel about what you know.-**Jim Rohn**

—

The most important thing in communication is hearing what isn't said.-**Peter Drucker**

—

Of all of our inventions for mass communication, pictures still speak the most universally understood language.-**Walt Disney**

—

First learn the meaning of what you say, and then speak.-**Epictetus**

—

Fill your paper with the breathings of your heart.-**William Wordsworth**

—

Communication works for those who work at it.-**John Powell**

—

Speak clearly, if you speak at all; carve every word before you let it fall.-**Oliver Wendell Holmes, Sr.**

Questions

Before you start some work, always ask yourself three questions – Why am I doing it, What the results might be and Will I be successful. Only when you think deeply and find satisfactory answers to these questions, go ahead.-**Chanakya**

—

To raise new questions, new possibilities, to regard old problems from a new angle, requires creative imagination and marks real advance in science.-**Albert Einstein**

—

I don't pretend we have all the answers. But the questions are certainly worth thinking about.-**Arthur C. Clarke**

—

The wise man doesn't give the right answers, he poses the right questions.-**Claude Levi-Strauss**

—

Culture makes people understand each other better. And if they understand each other better in their soul, it is easier to overcome the economic and political barriers. But first they have to understand that their neighbour is, in the end, just like them, with the same problems, the same questions.-**Paulo Coelho**

FAITH

Sometimes on a day during which nothing seems to happen everything gets way better. You just need a little more time to see the manifestation. Have a little faith. I go to work, The Universe (www.tut.com)

Faith is the strength by which a shattered world shall emerge into the light.-Helen Keller

—

To be a champ you have to have faith in yourself when no one else will.-Sugar Ray Robinson

—

Faith consists in believing when it is beyond the power of reason to believe.-Voltaire

—

Faith is not something to grasp, it is a state to grow into.-Mahatma Gandhi

—

We are twice armed if we fight with faith.-Plato

Hunger

—

I like to feel the butterflies in the stomach, I like to go home and have a restless night and wonder how I'm going to be able to accomplish this feat, get jittery. That hunger and those butterflies in the stomach are very essential for all creative people.-Amitabh Bachchan

—

It seems to me we can never give up longing and wishing while we are thoroughly alive. There are certain things we feel to be beautiful and good, and we must hunger after them.-George Eliot

—

Some people are born with very little; some are fortunate enough to have it all. When I grew up, we didn't have much. I had to hustle to get what I wanted... but I had that hunger for more. I didn't always make the right choices, but I learned from my mistakes.-Curtis Jackson

—

We have a hunger of the mind which asks for knowledge of all around us, and the more we gain, the more is our desire; the more we see, the more we are capable of seeing.- Maria Mitchell

---

Failure

Every adversity, every failure and every heartache carries with it the Seed of an equivalent or a greater Benefit. - Napoleon Hill

—

Success is the result of perfection, hard work, learning from failure, loyalty, and persistence. Colin Powell

—

It's fine to celebrate success but it is more important to heed the lessons of failure. Bill Gates

—

I can accept failure, everyone fails at something. But I can't accept not trying. Michael Jordan

---

Thoughts

Excellence is an art won by training and habituation. We do not act rightly because we have virtue or excellence, but we rather have those because we have acted rightly. We are what we repeatedly do. Excellence, then, is not an act but a habit. -Aristotle

Relentless, repetitive self-talk is what changes our self-image. -Denis Waitley

---

Gratitude

'Thank you' is the best prayer that anyone could say. I say that one a lot. Thank you expresses extreme gratitude, humility, understanding. Alice Walker

—

Gratitude is the healthiest of all human emotions. The more you express gratitude for what you have, the more likely you will have even more to express gratitude for. Zig Ziglar -
No person was ever honored for what he received. Honor has been the reward for what he gave. – Calvin Coolidge

—

Happiness cannot be traveled to, owned, earned, worn or consumed. Happiness is the spiritual experience of living every minute with love, grace, and gratitude. Denis Waitley

—

Develop an attitude of gratitude, and give thanks for everything that happens to you, knowing that every step forward is a step toward achieving something bigger and better than your current situation. Brian Tracy

—

Kindness

Kindness is the language which the deaf can hear and the blind can see. **–Mark Twain**

—

A warm smile is the universal language of kindness. **–William Arthur Ward**

—

A little thought and a little kindness are often worth more than a great deal of money. –**John Ruskin**

Smile

The real man smiles in trouble, gathers strength from distress, and grows brave by reflection.-**Thomas Paine**

If you smile when no one else is around, you really mean it.-**Andy Rooney**

A smile is a curve that sets everything straight.-**Phyllis Diller**

Smiling is definitely one of the best beauty remedies. If you have a good sense of humor and a good approach to life, that's beautiful.-**Rashida Jones**

Colors are the smiles of nature.-**Leigh Hunt**

The happiness of life is made up of minute fractions – the little, soon forgotten charities of a kiss or a smile, a kind look or heartfelt compliment.-**Samuel Taylor Coleridge**

There's nothing I value more than the closeness of friends and family, a smile as I pass someone on the street.-**Willie Stargell**

The Best Makeup Is Your Smile. - **J. Johnson**

Excuses

—

Using the power of decision gives you the capacity to get past any excuse to change any and every part of your life in an instant. Tony Robbins

—

An excuse becomes an obstacle in your journey to success when it is made in place of your best effort or when it is used as the object of the blame. Bo Bennett

—

Most people don't have that willingness to break bad habits. They have a lot of excuses and they talk like victims. Carlos Santana

—

I attribute my success to this - I never gave or took any excuse. Florence Nightingale

—

Hold yourself responsible for a higher standard than anybody expects of you. Never excuse yourself. Henry Ward Beecher

—

Visualization

–

What I think a lot of great marathon runners do is envision crossing that finish line. Visualization is critical. But for me, I set a lot of little goals along the way to get my mind off that overwhelming goal of 26.2 miles. I know I've got to get to 5, and

12, and 16, and then I celebrate those little victories along the way. Bill Rancic

—

Visualization – it's been huge for me. Your mind doesn't know the difference between imagination and reality. You can't always practice perfectly – my fingers will play a little bit out of tune, or my dance moves might not be as sharp – but in my mind, I can practice perfectly. Lindsey Stirling

—

Visualization is daydreaming with a purpose. Bo Bennett

—

Visualize this thing that you want, see it, feel it, believe in it. Make your mental blue print, and begin to build. Robert Collier

---

Meaning

We are at our very best, and we are happiest, when we are fully engaged in work we enjoy on the journey toward the goal we've established for ourselves. It gives meaning to our time off and comfort to our sleep. It makes everything else in life so wonderful, so worthwhile. Earl Nightingale

—

Without continual growth and progress, such words as improvement, achievement, and success have no meaning. Benjamin Franklin

—

To live is to suffer, to survive is to find some meaning in the suffering. Friedrich Nietzsche

—

Hero

If the Constitution was a movie, the Preamble would be the trailer, the First Amendment the establishing shot, the 13th the crowd pleaser and the 14th the ultimate hero scene. Henry Rollins

—

In order to become a hero you have to make sacrifices. John Barrowman

—

I think of a hero as someone who understands the degree of responsibility that comes with his freedom. Bob Dylan

—

I'm saying to be a hero is means you step across the line and are willing to make a sacrifice, so heroes always are making a sacrifice. Heroes always take a risk. Heroes always deviant. Heroes always doing something that most people don't and we want to change - I want to democratise heroism to say any of us can be a hero. Philip Zimbardo

—

A hero is born among a hundred, a wise man is found among a thousand, but an accomplished one might not be found even among a hundred thousand men. Plato

—

Humor Laughter

I live in a neighborhood so bad that you can get shot while getting shot. Chris Rock

—

My psychiatrist told me I was crazy and I said I want a second opinion. He said okay, you're ugly too. Rodney Dangerfield

—

I don't accept the status quo. I do accept Visa, MasterCard, or American Express. Stephen Colbert

—

People say New Yorkers can't get along. Not true. I saw two New Yorkers, complete strangers, sharing a cab. One guy took the tires and the radio; the other guy took the engine. David Letterman

—

There is no such thing as an impartial jury because there are no impartial people. There are people that argue on the web for hours about who their favorite character on 'Friends' is. Jon Stewart

—

Now they show you how detergents take out bloodstains, a pretty violent image there. I think if you've got a T-shirt with a bloodstain all over it, maybe laundry isn't your biggest problem. Maybe you should get rid of the body before you do the wash. Jerry Seinfeld

—

My grandmother started walking five miles a day when she was sixty. She's ninety-seven now, and we don't know where the hell she is. Ellen DeGeneres

—

Trying on pants is one of the most humiliating things a man can suffer that doesn't involve a woman. Larry David

—

Oh, you hate your job? Why didn't you say so? There's a support group for that. It's called everybody, and they meet at the bar. Drew Carey

—

A day without sunshine is like, you know, night. Steve Martin

—

If my father had hugged me even once, I'd be an accountant right now. Ray Romano

—

Behind every great man is a woman rolling her eyes. Jim Carrey

—

Yeah, I think that's sort of the American way. And it's also the Polish way, it turns out. Bill Murray

—

If you want to make an audience laugh, you dress a man up like an old lady and push her down the stairs. —If you want to make comedy writers laugh, you push an actual old lady down the stairs. Tina Fey

—

Thank you… fantasy football draft, for letting me know that even in my fantasies, I am bad at sports. Jimmy Fallon

—

Laughter heals all wounds, and that's one thing that everybody shares. No matter what you're going through, it makes you forget about your problems. I think the world should keep laughing. Kevin Hart

—

My mother and father were very strange people. They tried to be funny which is always very sad to me. Jonathan Winters

—

He who hesitates is poor. Mel Brooks

—

Carpe per diem – seize the check. You know the difference between a tornado and divorce in the south? Nothing! Someone is losing a trailer. Robin Williams

—

You know what it's like having five kids? Imagine you're drowning. And someone hands you a baby. Jim Gaffigan

—

Some people say funny things, but I say things funny. Don Rickles

—

When I was a boy, I laid in my twin size bed, wondering where my brother was. Mitch Hedberg

—

WORRY

—

Our fatigue is often caused not by work, but by worry, frustration and resentment.-Dale Carnegie

—

Worry is a technique you created to fill the moments of your life. –Wayne Dyer

—

Don't worry about the world coming to an end today. It is already tomorrow in Australia.-Charles M. Schulz

—

You're only here for a short visit. Don't hurry, don't worry. And be sure to smell the flowers along the way.-Walter Hagen

Response/Reaction

When we meet real tragedy in life, we can react in two ways – either by losing hope and falling into self-destructive habits, or by using the challenge to find our inner strength. Thanks to the teachings of Buddha, I have been able to take this second way.-Dalai Lama

—

People respond in accordance to how you relate to them. If you approach them on the basis of violence, that's how they'll react. But if you say, 'We want peace, we want stability,' we can then do a lot of things that will contribute towards the progress of our society.-Nelson Mandela

—

What if you believed or responded to situations that there were no 'bad' experiences? Isn't it true that no matter what you go through in life….EVERY experience provides for something of value if you look for it? – Tony Robbins

—

The possibilities are numerous once we decide to act and not react.-George Bernard Shaw

—

Every human has four endowments – self-awareness, conscience, independent will and creative imagination. These give us the ultimate human freedom… The power to choose, to respond, to change.-Stephen Covey

—

Our lives are not determined by what happens to us but how we react to what happens, not by what life brings us but the attitude we bring to life.-Wade Boggs

—

Life is 10% what happens to you and 90% how you react to it.-Charles R. Swindoll

---

Learning

Education is what remains after one has forgotten what one has learned in school.-**Albert Einstein**

—

Tell me and I forget. Teach me and I remember. Involve me and I learn.-**Benjamin Franklin**

—

A wise man can learn more from a foolish question than a fool can learn from a wise answer.-**Bruce Lee**

—

He who learns but does not think, is lost! He who thinks but does not learn is in great danger.-**Confucius**

—

He who would learn to fly one day must first learn to stand and walk and run and climb and dance; one cannot fly into flying.-**Friedrich Nietzsche**

—

There is no end to education. It is not that you read a book, pass an examination, and finish with education. The whole of life, from the moment you are born to the moment you die, is a process of learning.-**Jiddu Krishnamurti**

—

—

Leadership and learning are indispensable to each other.-**John F. Kennedy**

—

It is paradoxical that many educators and parents still differentiate between a time for learning and a time for play without seeing the vital connection between them.-**Leo Buscaglia**

—

I never learned from a man who agreed with me.-**Robert A. Heinlein**

—

Learning never exhausts the mind.-**Leonardo da Vinci**

—

Prepare for the unknown by studying how others in the past have coped with the unforeseeable and the unpredictable.-**George S. Patton**

—

It's what you learn after you know it all that counts.-**John Wooden**

—

CERTAINTY

The quest for certainty blocks the search for meaning. Uncertainty is the very condition to impel man to unfold his powers.-**Erich Fromm**

The demand for certainty is one which is natural to man, but is nevertheless an intellectual vice.-**Bertrand Russell**

One must verify or expel his doubts, and convert them into the certainty of Yes or No.-**Thomas Carlyle**

Although our intellect always longs for clarity and certainty, our nature often finds uncertainty fascinating.-**Carl von Clausewitz**

There is no certainty; there is only adventure.-**Roberto Assagioli**

Certainty is the mother of quiet and repose, and uncertainty the cause of variance and contentions.-**Edward Coke**

Facts matter not at all. Perception is everything. It's certainty.-**Stephen Colbert**

WHY

There are two great days in a person's life – the day we are born and the day we discover why.-William Barclay
—

Slow down and enjoy life. It's not only the scenery you miss by going to fast – you also miss the sense of where you are going and why.-Eddie Cantor

FEAR

Courage is never to let your actions be influenced by your fears.-**Arthur Koestler**
—

Love is what we were born with. Fear is what we learned here.-**Marianne Williamson**
—

Fear is static that prevents me from hearing myself.-**Samuel Butler**

—

To him who is in fear everything rustles.-**Sophocles**

—

Fear is excitement without breath.-**Robert Heller**

—

No good work is ever done while the heart is hot and anxious and fretted.-**Olive Schreiner**

—

If you can change your state of mind, then the fear will disappear. You need to change from a state of fear or uncertainty, to a state of certainty.-**Tony Robbins**

—

We gain strength, and courage, and confidence by each experience in which we really stop to look fear in the face... we must do that which we think we cannot.-**Eleanor Roosevelt**

—

Courage is resistance to fear, mastery of fear, not absence of fear.-**Mark Twain**

—

I learned that courage was not the absence of fear, but the triumph over it. The brave man is not he who does not feel afraid, but he who conquers that fear.-**Nelson Mandela**

Risk

The biggest risk is not taking any risk... In a world that changing really quickly, the only strategy that is guaranteed to fail is not taking risks. Mark Zuckerberg

—

The risk of a wrong decision is preferable to the terror of indecision. Maimonides

—

If you are not willing to risk the unusual, you will have to settle for the ordinary. Jim Rohn

For more Words or to join the conversation, visit www. onewebstrategy.com or email me at JIMFREYWTLB@gmail.com

Printed in the United States
By Bookmasters